Suomenlinna // Gropius

Paula Kramer

Two Contemplations on Body, Movement

and Intermateriality

tp

SUOMENLINNA

Was macht sie? Sie macht Yoga! Was macht
sie? Sie schläft! Was macht sie? Sie
tut als ob sie schläft! Was macht
sie? Fragst du sie? Ja, frag du sie!
(06.03.2017)

Introduction

What is she doing? She is doing yoga! What is she doing? She is sleeping! What is she doing? She is pretending to sleep! Will you ask her? Yes, you ask her! (06.03.2017)

A conversation between children, approaching whilst I practise. Practise what? Movement. Movement in relationship. Dance. Intermateriality. Choreography. Life. Living.

Based on extended site-based research (2016-2019), conducted in the framework of a post-doc at Uniarts Helsinki's Centre for Artistic Research (CfAR), this book opens into what I was doing: researching intermateriality, through bodily practice. Working on two sites, one here, one there, one in Helsinki, one in Berlin.

It speaks to and from the question I ask myself: how does movement and choreography emerge in collaboration with site? More specifically: how do bodies, sites, materials, organisms, history, tuning, weather, training, occurrences (and more) intermingle and speak, bringing forth what we later might call movement, dance or choreography? Not alone, next to or alongside each other, but together, in intermateriality (a term I turn to later and unfold in this book).

I engage with the touchable, tangible yes, but also with the less graspable, less knowable. Summa summarum: How can I (you, we) dance here (anywhere) – so that the aliveness of everything past and present can surface and shimmer?

Read both ways.   Take turns!

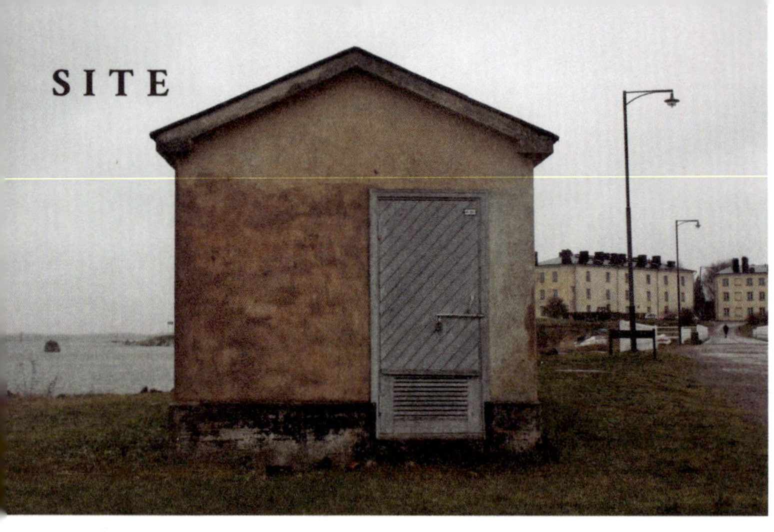

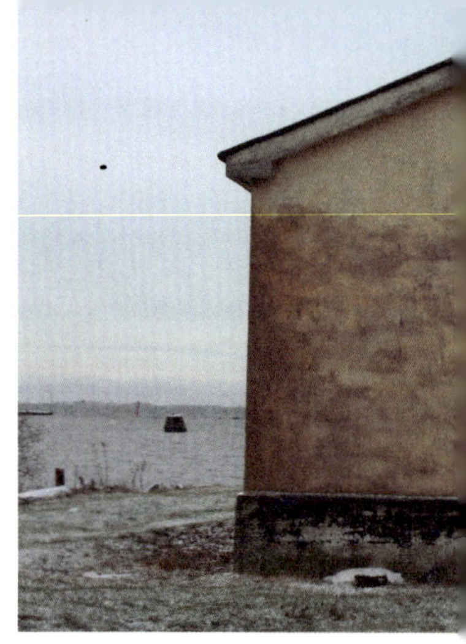

11.11.2017

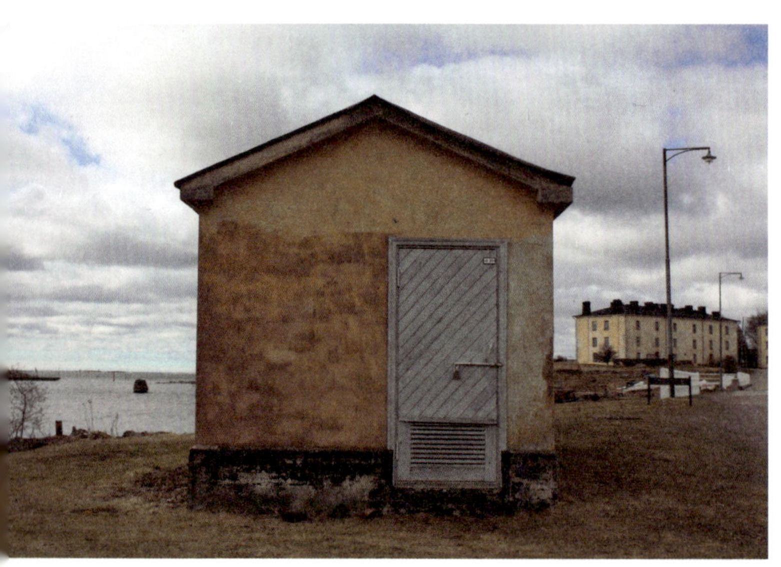

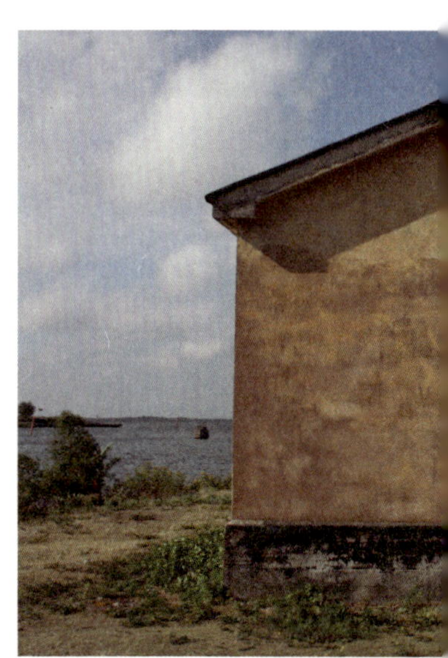

21.04.2018

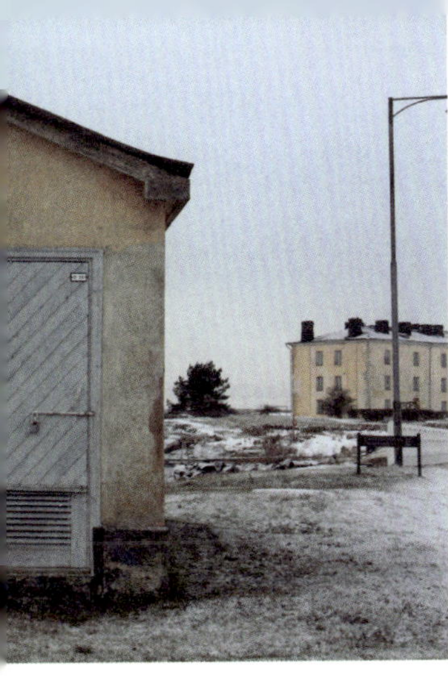

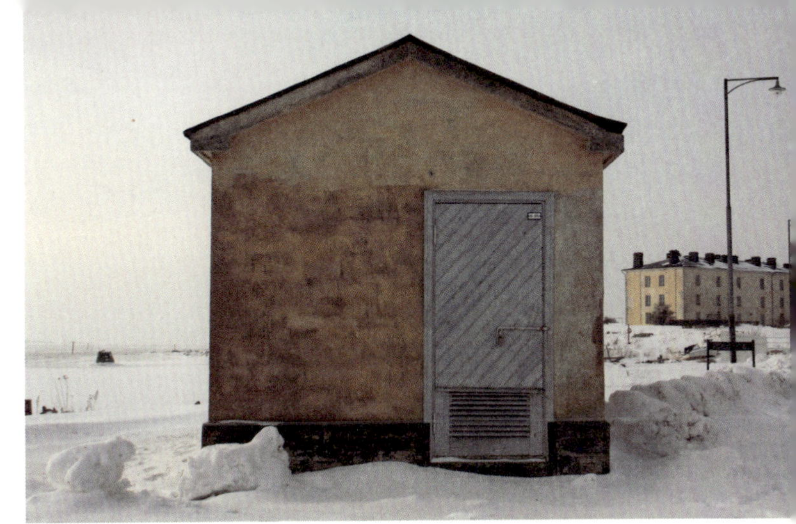

28.01.2018

11.02.2018

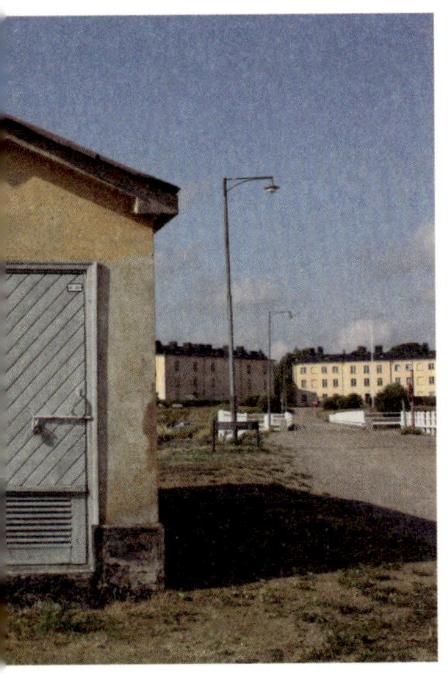

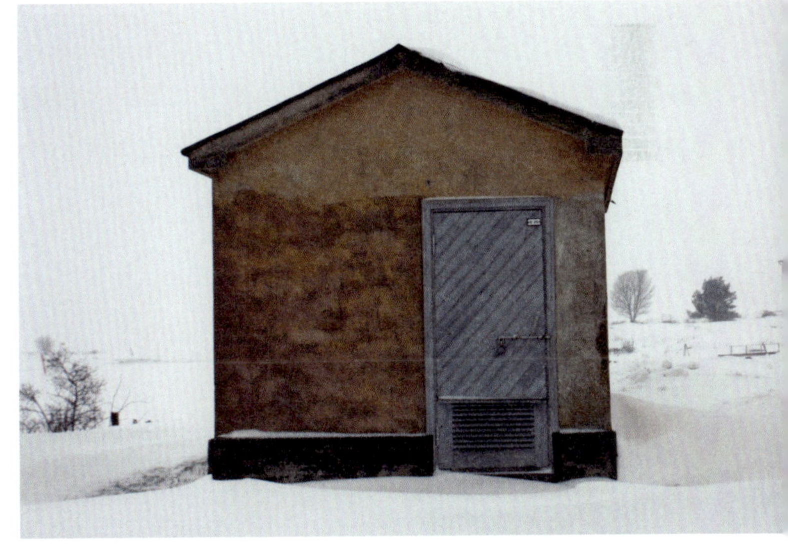

28.07.2018

29.01.2019

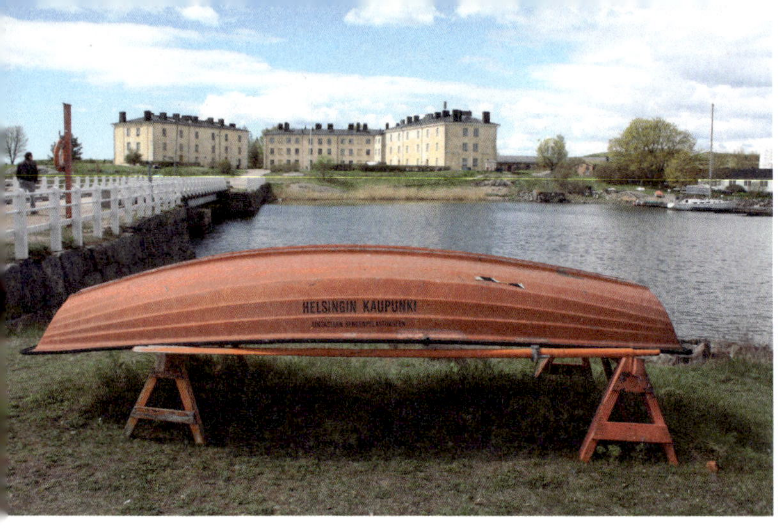
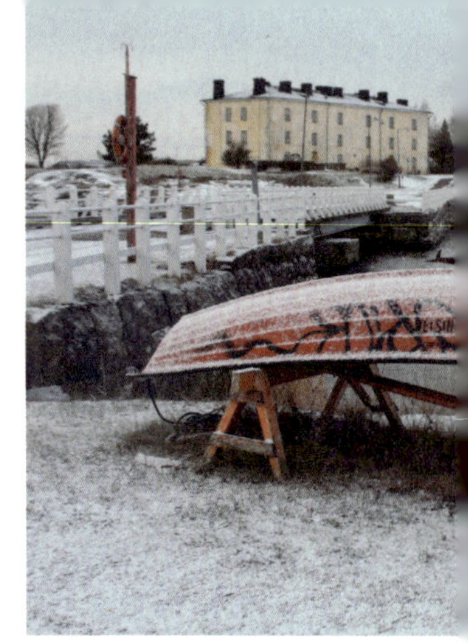

26.05.2017

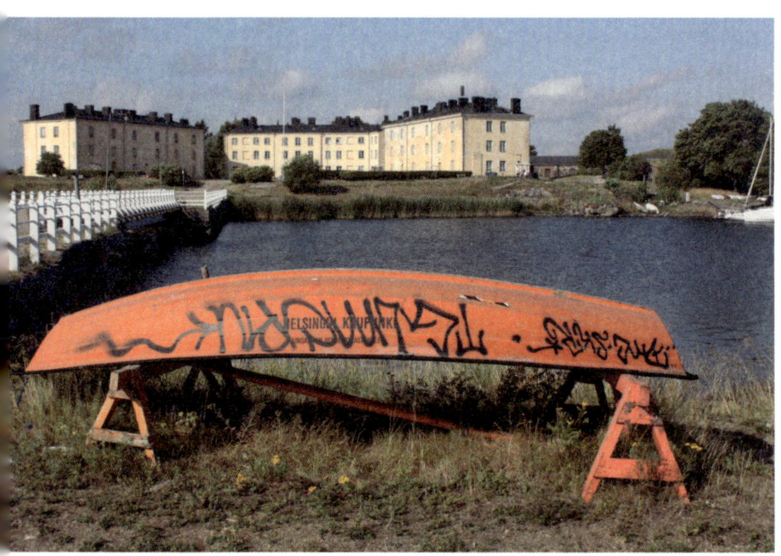
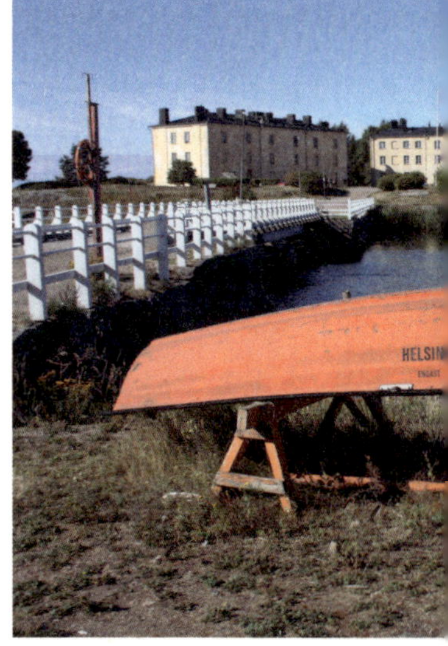

28.07.2018

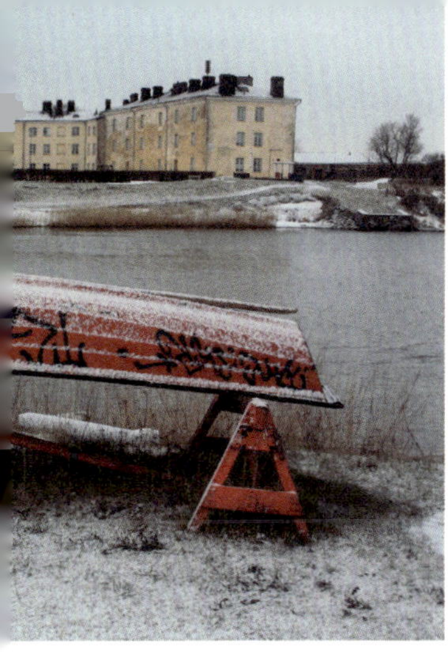

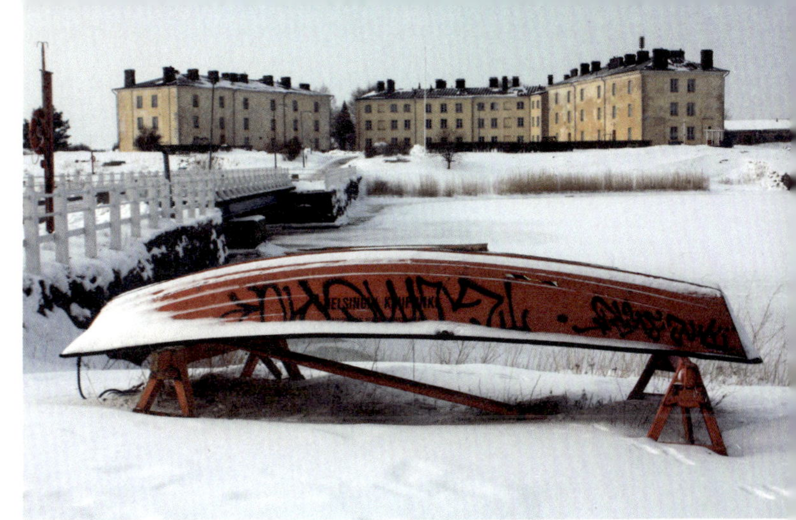

28.01.2018

17.02.2018

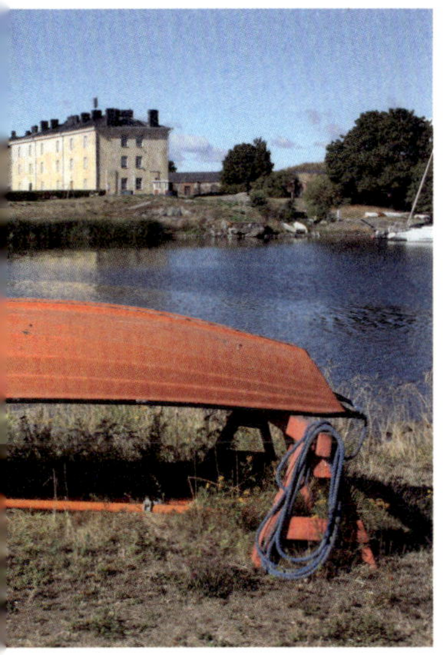

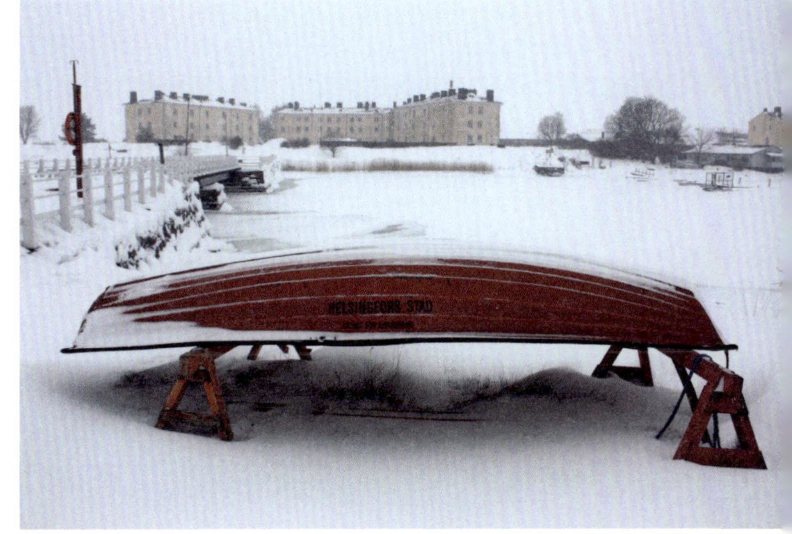

14.08.2018

29.01.2019

Rocks lying quietly in the water, iced
elephant backs, whales. Red and black the
rock, white the ice, green the moss, grey
the sea and the sky.
(18.01.2017)

Seagulls flying past without hurry, everything
has ease, expression, pace. I see surface
today, skin and dryness.
(29.05.2018)

So much going on here, always. Even if
seemingly nothing happens. This world, so
alive. I walk and am struck by the amount
of movement and colour and motion and energy
or potential or something like that.
(14.11.2018)

This has become my place in so many ways,
and yet it is not at all.
(18.05.2019)

SUOMENLINNA
– On Your Rocks I Lie

//Paula Kramer

"Would you know of a site that has, well – some rocks; that is maybe by the water, easy to reach and not too populated?" Something like this I must have asked my Suomenlinna hosts Saarajohanna and Miro in December 2016, when I began to look for a site to work with. I was very new to Finland, very new to Suomenlinna, a temporary guest for an envisaged three-year period, coming and going in the frame of a post-doctoral research position at Uniarts Helsinki. I had recently performed alongside a large slab of granite and a stonemason as part of the UK-based research network 'Rock/Body'. And I had moved with, around, between rocks for many years before – in the Catalan Pyrenees, on the Jurassic Coast in southwest England and in Scotland also.[1] So in all the newness of Finland, of Helsinki, of Suomenlinna, I was looking for one thing familiar, something to connect with, somewhere to start. And rock is very present here: landing in Vantaa the first time, taking the train towards the city, rock is the first thing I notice – the railway tracks cutting through enormous bedrock left and right, huge slates, sometimes secured with wire constructions. This city was rock, is rock, is built on rock, has rock sticking out everywhere, like an elbow, a knee-joint, a knuckle.

Like sleeping giants the rock is lying. I see it immediately upon arrival, how it calls. In open form, blunt, coarse, untamed. Very present, large, powerful, in the middle of the urban environment. (12.12.2016)

1. Kramer, Paula (2012): 'Bodies, Rivers, Rocks and Trees: Meeting agentic materiality in contemporary outdoor dance practices', in *Performance Research: A Journal of the Performing Arts*, 17:4, pp. 83-91; Kramer, Paula (2015): *Dancing Materiality. A Study of Agency and Confederations in Contemporary Outdoor Dance Practices.* PhD Thesis. Coventry University, Centre for Dance Research.

In these early days I was thinking of a site in the city or somewhere in the archipelago. I had no sense of what was anywhere, apart from a very few landmarks: Kauppatori, the Suomenlinna ferry, Hakaniemie and Haapaniemenkatu 6, where the Theatre Academy and my temporary work desk were located.

"Well yes, around here" they replied, shrugging, slightly bewildered and very matter of fact. Surprised that I did not seem to notice the obvious: that I was on an island formed by age-old bedrock, surrounded by water, of course, and very easy to reach. Here.

That Suomenlinna had become my occasional and temporary home was due only to random and lucky circumstances and the generous Kuru family, who took me in each time I came. I think it must have been the second time I stayed with them, and 'here' had not really configured itself as a possibility in my mind at all. All that I had seen of Suomenlinna thus far was an artificial Disneyland type site, full of museums and tourists. Not that I would exclude working in constructed or tourist sites per se, but this one seemed so full of people that it felt impossible to work here. I felt doubtful that I could begin to move here in the very simple ways in which I tend to begin; ways that have nothing to do with performance and that, to the untrained eye, might sometimes look like I might be needing help. What is she doing, lying, crawling there? Why is she standing slightly bent? Is she chanting to the sea or is something wrong? I felt too vulnerable to expose myself to flocks of tourists in this way, but, encouraged by my hosts' very simple and immediate gesture of – "well yes, around here" – I did realize that it was worth taking a closer look at this place of fame and flocking. Starting without having to further travel anywhere, starting right here, right now, was the best thing that could have happened anyway. So I take a first walk on December 16th, 2016, a quiet day. All around, all around, all around. All around the five Suomenlinna islands that are connected by bridges – Kustaanmiekka, Susisaari, Iso Mustasaari, Pikku Mustasaari, Länsi-Mustasaari. Two further islands form part of this group, Lonna and Särkkä, but both can only be reached by boat, so I exclude them from my roaming. I take a very few photos with an old, feeble phone, and write down a first few notes. I remember seeing many of Suomenlinna's relevant sites that day (the dry dock, the King's Gate and so on), and also spending quite some time behind a former army barracks and prison camp, now art gallery and project space for HIAP (Helsinki International Artist Programme) and the Nordic Culture Point. One possible place I consider working in, is the quiet, rocky coastline right behind this long rosy-red building.

It is cold but not freezing, beautifully sunny, sky wide open, light almost extreme. The ground is hard, frozen. Though on the whole not much ice, no snow and temperatures not much below zero, if at all. Warm in the sun. I walk and I walk and I see – the submarine, the defence mounds, old cannons, quiet buildings. A fortress! It feels somewhat surreal. To be here. To walk here. To live here. To think of dancing here. Dancing what? (16.12.2016)

I move onwards, and in the end find Länsi-Mustasaari, the 'Western (Länsi) Black (Musta) Island (Saari)', abbreviated by the islanders as Länskäri. I am welcomed by rocks, space, birds, trees, shrubs, wind, light and quietness. Only very few houses, a row of gardens and behind these what I would consider the wildest and least populated zone of the central Suomenlinna islands. "Here I can work!" – this is immediately obvious. The site is large, offering several possible places to work in, varied in terms of height, vegetation, coastline, size of rock, colour of rock, exposure to wind and so on.

There are pathways all around but very few people on them, especially at this time of year. An occasional dog walker, an adventurous tourist, residents on a walk, families out and about – but on this particular first day I meet almost no-one and am immediately taken by the site.

> *At the end, tip of the island, I huddle into rock, lie on my side, happily moving my hands, fingers, finally arms. The light is spectacular; every tiny fibre of my glove is glowing against the light. I crawl up the rock and standing up there I start to sing. From deep in the throat somewhere, directly through the nose is what it feels like. It is almost not me. Thereafter I see the place differently arranged in its three dimensions, this boulder there crouching like me and the sea that I did not hear before speaking back to me in the quiet. (16.12.2016)*

From this day onwards I come back here, again and again, sometimes once a month, sometimes twice and sometimes less. What I write down I remember very well; other things I don't find in my notes but still remember – like walking around the margins of Länskäri, taking the long way around, before and behind the gardens, a zone I later don't explore further and that I only cross occasionally when I change my way of walking to or from what then becomes the site I focus on.

With time I develop a routine way of walking to and from this site, but this takes a while and there are many variations. From where I live I can choose the back route past the island kindergarten or walk past the church on the most popular tourist highway. I can weave my way closer to water and boats or further away, I can come up to the small island supermarket from behind or walk past the ferry and its main entrance. It all depends on how much time I have, how much equipment I am carrying, how leisurely or hurried I feel, what the weather says. After the bridge to Pikku Mustasaari, the island that hosts most of the current military buildings, I have to take a left to reach Länskäri. Most of the pathways on this island have trespassing forbidden signs, but it is possible to cross one military courtyard, which I sometimes do.

In the beginning, I often take a right after the last bridge to Länskäri, walk past the playground and enter the site through what I would later come to consider the back end. Walking in a circle, coming out the other side after practice. With more routine I almost always take a left and return the same way, walking past the yellow houses where both Saarajohanna and Miro used to live, long ago, when they started out on this island.

Shared clothes lines are strung up behind these houses, bordered by bountiful gardens and rosehip bushes. Once this civilized zone is left behind, a wild mini-hinterland opens. It begins with a big tree, marking the 'entrance', a public toilet on the right-hand side, waste containers on the left and a slightly hilly pathway leading in, first down, bordered by shrubs and grasses, and then slightly up again, to the big boulders, the large slabs, the wide slates of rock, of rock, of rock and more trees and grassy hills further up.

This Site Speaks

The site I work with is marked with a singular and noticeable guardian tree: an old birch with many witches' brooms (or tuulenpesä – wind's nest), a growth caused by the fungus *Taphrina betulina*. Especially in winter, the tree looks like it has movement, many twirls in its crown, or nests or brooms, yes, how fitting the names that I learn much later from my mother and Saarajohanna.

From here onwards I study: rock, sky, crust, shrubs, weather, animals, deep time, sea. Rock has form, rock has texture, rock has density, temperature, colour. Rock has movement, is movement. The sky has dimension, colour and wind. A hole in the clouds, layers, ruptures, some blue. The trees have small leaves, rustling, sometimes something metal goes ting-a-ling in the wind somewhere. The world speaks if I am ready to listen.

Roughly the site divides (in my mind) into an upper and a lower level. The lower level is mainly rock, opening towards the sea – large, dark, grey; also red, brown, ochre and many twirls, veins, rosy, white. Some trees also, shrubs, grasses. Cracks and ledges. Crevices filled with ice in the winter and violets in the early summer. A small rock pool, some puddles that fill regularly.

The upper level needs some clambering up to, is again a rock site but more inland, more shelter. Some sort of a platform up there, more mosses, lichens and many small birches. Grasses and green rolling hills even further inland – overgrown military structures. One old anti-aircraft gun towering prominently on one of the highest points.

The military history is omnipresent on Suomenlinna, a world-famous sea fortress of course, with an active naval academy to this day. Yet this militarized side of things seeps into my work less than I would have anticipated. Did I actively ignore it? Did it not resonate in my movement because the details are too unknown to me, the fate of Russians, Swedes and Finns, Whites and Reds not entwined with my immediate family history? I see the cannons, the gun, of course. I walk over and along the old defence mounds. I witness tourists investigating the remnants of former wars: *"I will shoot you with that bad ass cannon!!" (Two white men without shirts and bad posture shouting at each other, already gone). (23.07.2018)*

One anti-aircraft gun I always have in view, it always witnesses me. Part of my score emerges in dialogue with its prominence, its lines, its orientation. But I dialogue with something more general, universal here, rather than having a viscerally concrete experience of the military history of this site.

Seasons and Weather

Weather is my daily companion: ice, sun, clouds, rain, wind, rainbow, cold, snow, heat. In the winter I hear the crackling noise of ice on water; in May the softness of summer enraptures me. Ten drops of rain fall and my body arrives. Every day is incredibly distinct and in my notes I ask myself how we can expect to function the same every day when already two consecutive summer days are totally different from each other.

The weather changes quickly and extremely, it can be bright and sunny when I step out of the door and grey and windy with a rough sea once I arrive on site. Sometimes it is so cold that my hands hurt and stillness seems to be the only movement possible. Sometimes it is so hot that I can only work very early and very late in the day.

A surprising number of people hang out here in summer, especially in the evenings. Here two, and there two, and one with a hammock and one walking past. Not exactly many... but: many more than at other times. In the winter the whole landscape changes dramatically with snow and ice coming and then melting again.

This going back and forth throughout winter, this coming and going of an icy skin, is an indicator of climate change, I am told. On a phone I am shown a photo from the 1980s that is passed around, the ice so thick between Suomenlinna and the mainland that a car drives over it, part of a procession of people going back and forth. Today the ferry channel is kept open throughout anyway, with passenger numbers much increased.

In the beginning the changing ice puzzles me, I have problems recognizing places that I had already moved in.

> *Basically, I am totally perplexed. The ice has gone. Though not unexpected, I hardly recognize the place from yesterday. The site where I had moved, that I had moved in, the ice that had moved with me, around me, is gone. The whole surface in front of me is just water. There is hardly any wind, just the water moving slightly, slushing, gushing against the rocks and the small glacier-like fields that are still left. This skin of the earth, or skin of the sea has melted. Yet the open water also has a surface, a skin, ever more tender, it would not carry me. (15.02.2017)*

Later that day, on the ferry, I reminisce that the skin of the sea is more sensitive than my own – reacting drastically, immediately to the change of temperature. Whilst I could also feel that it was getting warmer, I remain in the wider realm of cold, freezing; the air sharp against my skin. But the ice was already melting, reacting to the warmth immediately. Helpless in a way, entangled of course, maybe just doing what it was doing, changing its state of aggregation.

Only once is the site closed. Closed by winter, closed by snow, closed by wind. It is the winter after the performance, a fitting moment for me to not-enter, to retreat.

I am curious to see if this is real, I test the snow, but sink in way too deep. No footsteps beyond the public toilets (also closed). Same coming the other way. Road cleared up to a point, no footsteps beyond. A cat exploring, a little bit, here and there, but also not in the deep-deep snow.

It makes me happy to see that this site can be closed.

Companions

The second time I enter the site, I find hare bones and furry paws, frozen, by the guardian birch. I see them regularly in the first winter and sometimes pause next to them, next to the guarding tree, when I enter or exit the site. Until one day they are gone. On my farewell day on site I doze off on the large rocks and, briefly opening my eyes in between half-sleep, I see hare sitting next to the forlorn concrete pillar that marks my visual axis, towards the sea, out towards the sea. Close and fairy-tale-like and big. An arch from beginning to end. An under-current, almost forgotten. But then very present, with bones in the first winter and saying hello in the flesh at the very end.

There are many animals I cross paths with, companion species to this work. First and foremost: birds. Crows circle above me, magpies come along, seagulls fly past, sometimes swans, wagtails. Barnacle geese, arctic terns and eider ducks, according to the season. I sometimes meet a cat on my way, in winter and summer. A couple of eagle owls live on the islands; on our sauna evenings we can hear their dark eerie calls, never in my practice times though. A wren visits once. A young otter plays by my side in the water and among the rocks throughout my intensive rehearsal period leading up to performing in August 2018. Many ants bite me in the same phase. Sometimes, rarely, I see a snake.

On September 4th, 2017 the sea gifts me an intriguing object – a large, voluptuous, rosy pink buoy. *It is my day of finding many things,* I note: *Two birch boletus, two glasses, a handful of rhubarb, a small pack of pencil leads and one big buoy that I pull out of the water and onto the rock. (04.09.2017)*

Buoy becomes my love affair on this island, my steady friend, my companion in this whole endeavour. She sleeps in winter, moves with me in all other seasons, tossed by autumn winds in November.

Very small snowflakes continue to fall and I am drawn to the open rocks where I worked with the buoy, once upon a time. She is now lying sleeping covered with snow, I am not yet sure if I will wake her this time. (11.02.2018)

The island also gifts me a person, one of the educators running the island kindergarten. We meet in the first winter, she is walking with her dog and writes her name in the snow. I muse that I would trust her with my child (one, then) in any language, should the opportunity or necessity arise. So open, warm, friendly, steady. We see each other only very occasionally and in passing, but in the end she comes with a friend and a dancing child to see the final performance, for which I will be forever grateful. Apart from my hosts these are the only islanders that ever see the work.

And then there is rock, and rock, and rock. And colour of rock and texture of rock and density of rock – *I remember the rosy quartz, such delicate shades of white and pink, meeting lines of dark and grey and covered by mosses and lichen. Green and soft, incredibly soft, and hard and grey, and round patches. (27.01.2018)*

Suomenlinna significantly deepens my experiential base of being around and moving with rock(s). Building a relationship. Feeling a profound sense of being carried. I find immense satisfaction and comfort in lying positions – close to rock, form to form, so secure, so unmistaken. Diving deep, sinking deep, held in deep time. Rock is here, rock remains.

Very strong this feeling how everything happens to rock and it is (just) there. Water comes and goes, moss comes and goes and changes, animals come by, weather. Humans once lived here, time passes, rock remains. It has been and will be. The rest happens around it. (04.05.2018)

Sometimes I experience rock as incredibly hard. What am I doing? I wonder. How is this ever supposed to become anything but hard? And sometimes I experience rock as smooth, soft and friendly: *I find this incredibly soft rock place, so tender, so smooth. I can feel the earth breathing here, a soft fold with many lines – one possible place – to begin, to end? (23.07.2018)*

I relish the cracks and lines and colours that guide my movement. Scratches, break-offs and fissures telling stories of snow and ice that previously moved here. Water in all forms making places of comfort out of the rock, moulding rounds and seats and backs and curves. Patterns and colours telling stories of melted rock, of rock in movement itself, once having been soft, fluid, melted, somewhere deep down and under severe pressure. Rock has moved and it continues to move slowly. Circling around the globe more than once since the beginnings of planet Earth. These are maps that I can follow directly. The connection is visual – I see the fissures, cracks and lines. But the shapes, colours, forms and forces also seep directly into my body, re-emerging as movement.

Still und flach silent and smooth the site
is today, still und flach … it's a quiet day
and grey meets grey. Some birds sing and
I can hear and see the city across the water.
And many small birds now overhead, flocking
and chatting and quickly gone, onwards,
elsewhere.
(14.11.2018)

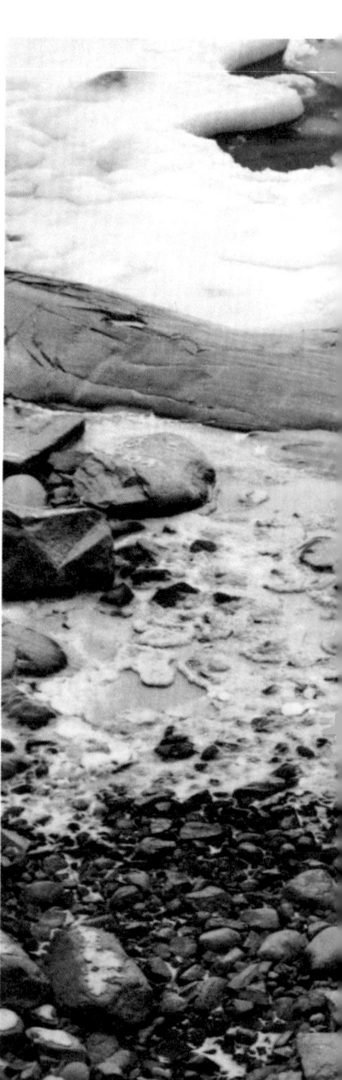

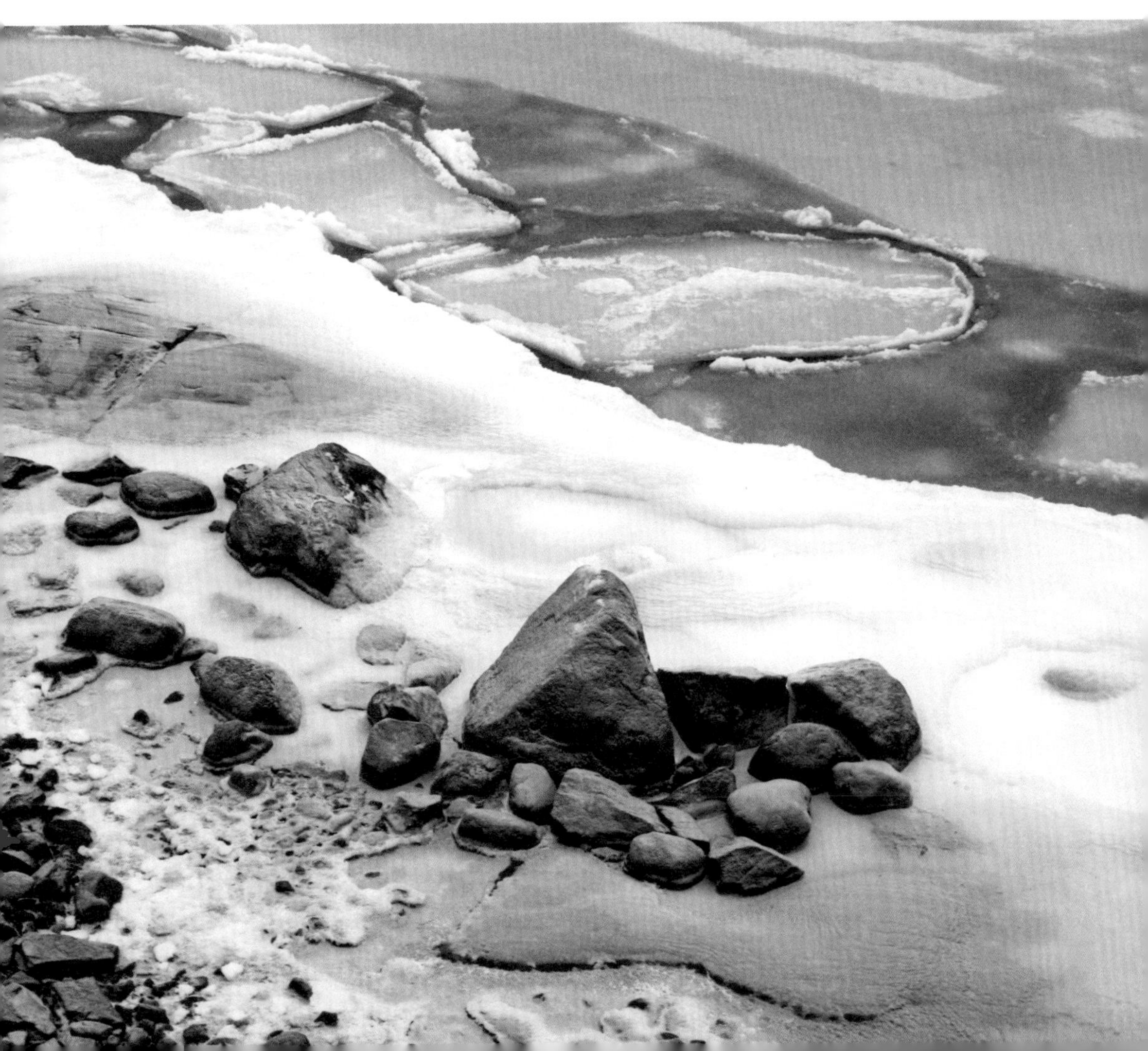

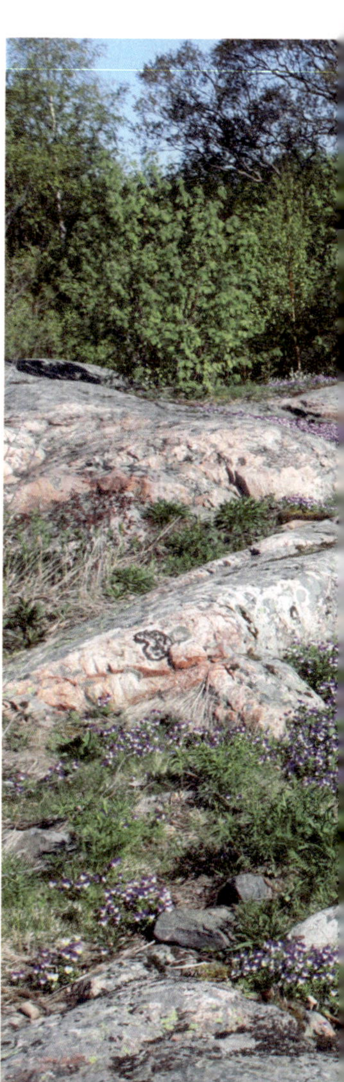

SITE

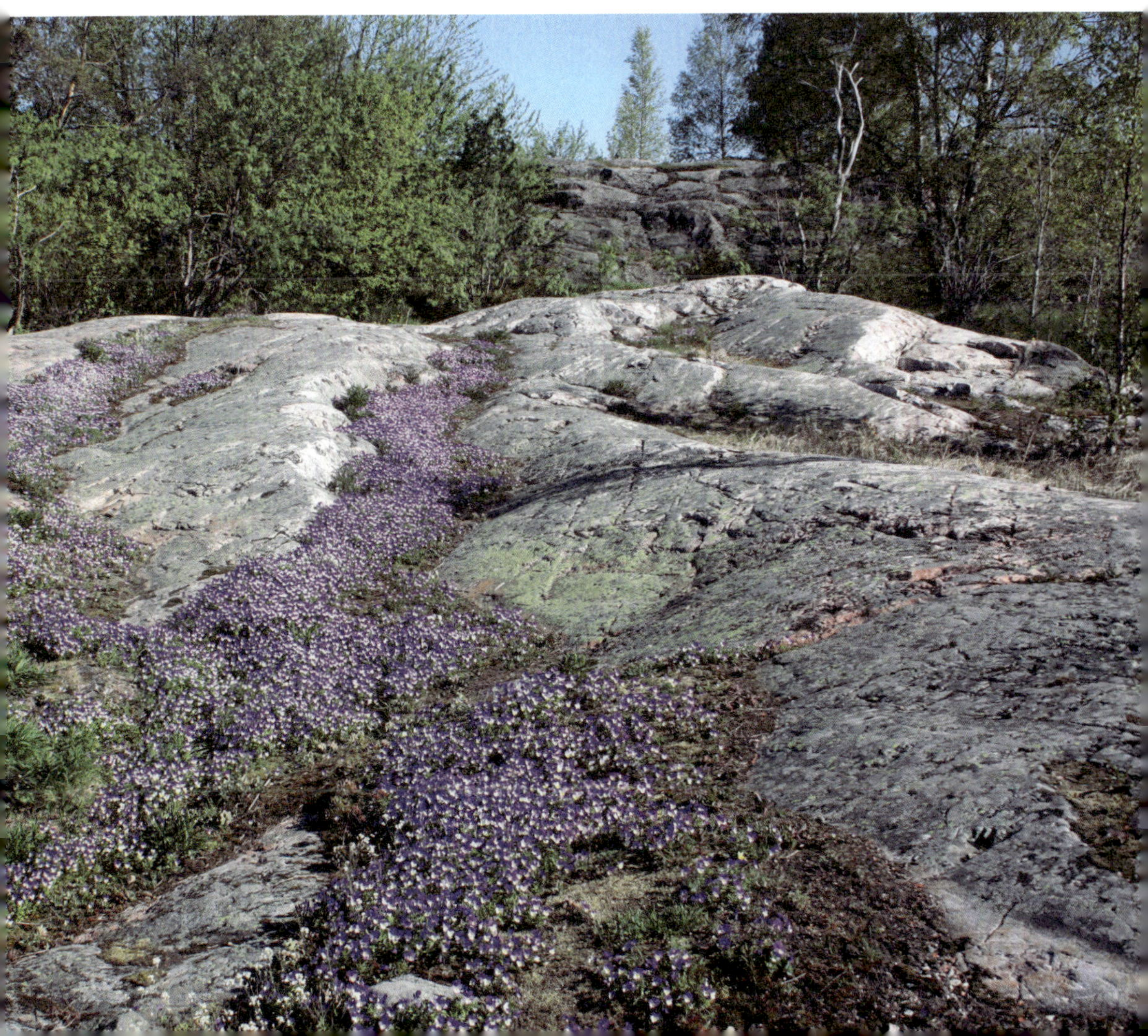

The Slippery Rocks of Suomenlinna

// Björn Kröger

The coastal rocks of Suomenlinna are dangerous in places. They may be slippery from the brine of the Baltic Sea and from the fine green algae growing on them. There are numerous cracks and hidden steps. Then, in other parts, the surface is smooth and polished like a large, precious silver plate. The everyday tourist and the weekend rambler, enjoying the view towards Helsinki city with its copper-roofed cathedral, the massive white ferry boats and the tiny little islands in between, needs to be careful not to stumble. The focus needs to be down with the rocks at all times.

These coastal rocks are the bedrock of Helsinki and the whole southern coast of Finland. They make it strikingly different from the landscape the traveller left when coming from further south, by ferry from Tallinn. Estonia has white limestone cliffs and soft sandy beaches. In Helsinki the coast is an endless assembly of rounded boulders thrown into the sea, smutted with algae and moss, and in places with the white faeces of gulls and geese. For me, a palaeontologist, these rocks are 'basement': crystalline, sterile, dead – a habitat hard to get through and the slippery ground for my weekend trips to Suomenlinna. Strange, mysterious, old. No fossils preserved, lots of shiny minerals instead, visible to the bare eye in many places. Colourful, indeed, with patches of dark grey, almost black, of pale rose, rusty brown or dirty bluish white, but also a kind of icy, impermeable, non-living fundament.

Finland was part of an ancient landmass for hundreds of millions of years, at least from the Devonian age onward – the time when the first higher plants expanded on land, around four hundred million years ago. At that time Finland was close to the equator and the climate was desert, dry and hot, and on top of

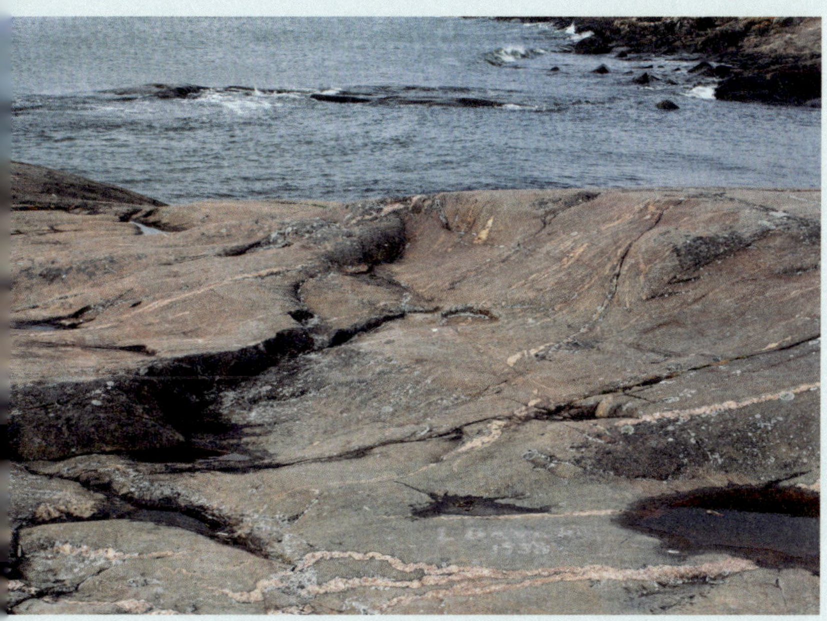

Bedrock of the southern coast of Finland

what is now crystalline surface rock, a few hundred metres of sandy and limy sediment still existed. Since the Devonian Period, rivers and the wind have eroded that younger rock away. Step by step exposing successively deeper and older strata, carving the crystals free that reflect the light today.

Then came the ice, just a few hundred thousand years ago. During this last ice age, the Pleistocene, glaciers amassed to a height of more than a kilometre above where we stand today at Suomenlinna. The glaciers gradually pressed their weight southwards, scratching away the last remaining parts of younger rocks, sending them as far as The Netherlands and central Germany. With a little luck one might find a Suomenlinna boulder in a construction pit at Potsdamer Platz, Berlin, brought some hundred thousand years ago by the ice.

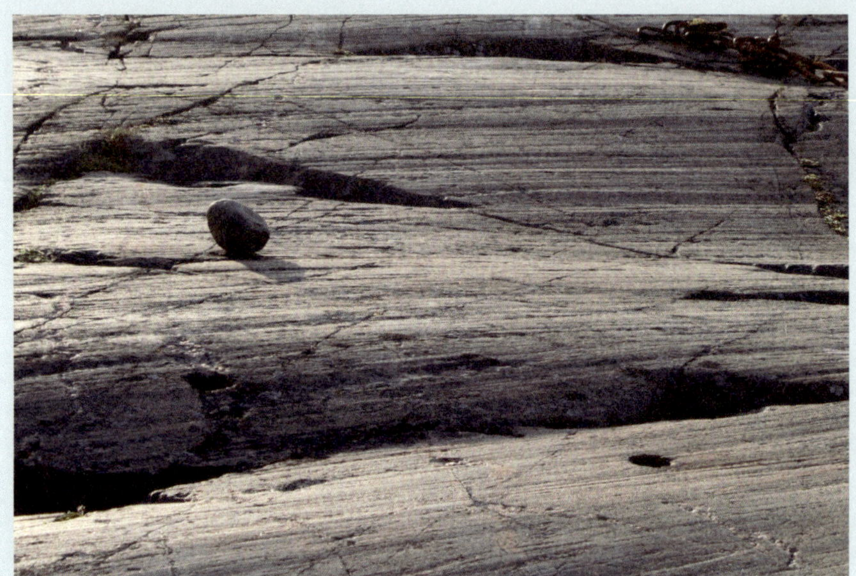

Pleistocene scratches

These Pleistocene scratches, found everywhere on the surfaces of the Suomenlinna cliffs, are reminders from that long lasting southward movement of the ice. Steadily, over tens of thousands of years and tens more thousands of years, for a time multiple times longer than any written history, the ice moved broken blocks of rock from the south to the north.

When the ice finally melted away, the sea came back. But the ice was heavy enough to bend the Earth's crust underneath Finland, Sweden and Norway. And like an elastic roof, the crust rebounds, slowly but irresistibly. This is the reason why even today the ground of Helsinki still rises a couple of centimetres per year, pushing the sea back again, as much as three metres per thousand years. Much of Suomenlinna was under the surface of the Baltic Sea just a millennium ago.

So what we see today is a surface of rocks shaped largely by the ice, some ten thousand years old, drowned by the sea and then exposed again, washed clean by the waves and every summer spotted by goose and seagull faeces. We see granite, as I would say as a palaeontologist. But this is not really correct, it is a kind of igneous rock which is a wild mix of patches of different types of rocks. I imagine it to be like a frozen dough of deep earth stuff imperfectly mixed by rock forming processes that I don't fully grasp. There are patches which are truly granite, composed of pale-pinkish feldspar, bluish-white quartz and shiny black mica. In other places the rock is black and looks like diabase, heavy dark minerals dominate, such as pyroxenes and amphiboles.

And there are these strange and beautiful dykes: massive cracks within the dark- or light-coloured patches that are filled with shiny masses of huge crystals. Individual crystals in the dykes sometimes reach the length of two of my

Frozen dough

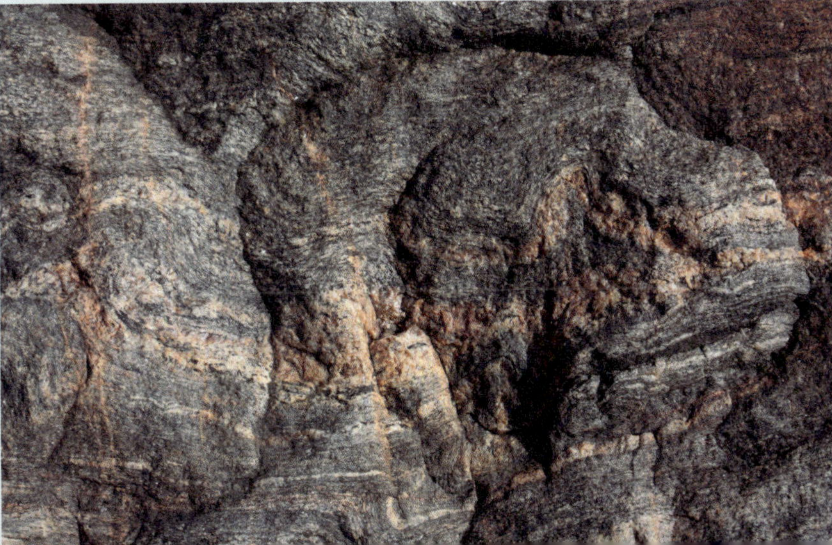

feet, or more. They are a milky-opaque pinkish colour, and large mica crystals look like silver or broken mirrors. The dykes are remnants of what geologists call pegmatite veins. We stand on the former tops of an ancient magma chamber. In this hellish place in the veins of the Earth's crust, light masses of rock melts concentrated and, over very long periods of geological time, persisted to form masses of beautiful crystals.

All this is now exposed, speaking of a time unimaginably old, testifying to the mountain-forming processes long, long ago. The time between the forming of the pale-coloured crystalline patches and the original formation of the surrounding dark rock masses may have easily been more than several hundred million years, some billion years ago. As if this is not enough, the dough below with its dykes and veins was heavily kneaded at a time, 1,900 million years ago, when mountains as high as the Himalayas stood above what is today Suomenlinna.

Southern Finland was then part of an old continent that connected what is now Denmark directly to an area which is today in the middle of Brazil's Amazon region. This old continent is named Rhodinia and lasted until only 700 million years ago. I must confess, this is getting somewhat confusing. One can easily get lost in these stories of times when animals where not yet around, and no moss grew, and no geese populated the place, nor weekend ramblers, who must take care not to stumble on the slippery ground.

Björn Kröger // is a curator of the Palaeontological Collections of the Finnish Museum of Natural History and docent at Helsinki University, Finland. He earned his PhD at the Freie Universität Berlin, Germany and worked in Germany, France and Sweden. He is an expert on the evolution of the oldest cephalopods. His current research focus is on the early evolution of large scale ecosystem engineering in the oceans. He also has an active interdisciplinary interest in how our knowledge about Earth's deep time is gained, narrated and used.

Islands in Time

//Annette Arlander

The performance site on the northwestern shore of the westernmost island of Suomenlinna was new to me, despite the fact that I have lived all my life in Helsinki and often visited the sea fortress too. Harakka Island, where I have had my studio since 1997, is visible from that shore, and used to belong to the same group of islands as the sea fortress, at least in a historical sense. It was funny to be introduced to a new perspective on that place by a visitor, but that is what often happens. We tend to stick to our ingrained routes and need somebody from elsewhere to show us how to look for other paths.

The history of Harakka Island, which I know better than the performance site, and which is much smaller, is for me a well-known example of the crossroads of influences that are present on the main Suomenlinna islands as well. Although the human history of the sea fortress involves more drama, more fighting and more suffering than the small and relatively unimportant Harakka island, they share the same general fate.

Suomenlinna Sea Fortress, today a UNESCO world heritage site, consists of several islands connected by bridges, including Länsi-Mustasaari, the performance site. Like the rest of the archipelago around Helsinki, it continues to rise slowly out of the sea, as it has been doing since the ice age. As a result, the islands are still expanding and geologically interesting, since various rock formations and traces of the ice are visible on the relatively bare cliffs of old bedrock. Human history is present in the fortifications and buildings dating from various times, the most recent of which are called the Swedish era, the Russian era and the Finnish era. The fortification work began after a decision by the Swedish parliament in 1747 involving what was then called Susiluodot (the wolf islets). The fortress was called Sveaborg, meaning Castle of Sweden, which became Viapori in Finnish, based on sounds easier to pronounce in Finnish (svea – via, borg – pori). Fortification works were never quite completed and in 1808, during the Russo-Swedish war, the commandant, C.O. Cronstedt, surrendered the fortress to the Russians, for unknown reasons. During the Russian era, after Sweden had lost Finland to Russia, the sea fortress was not part of the semi-autonomous Finnish Grand Duchy but was governed directly by Russia. In the summer of 1906, in the midst of revolutionary unrest, a mutiny erupted in the fortress, but was defeated in four days. The jokes claiming that the Russian revolution started on the islands probably stem from that mutiny. During the First World War the fortress was further strengthened to protect the Russian capital, St. Petersburg. Finland's independence and the Finnish Civil War in 1918 coincided with the Russian Revolution. Towards the end of the war, the Whites (nationalists) set up a prison camp on Viapori for 8,000 Reds (communist and other prisoners); many of them were executed and many died of disease due to the poor conditions in the fortress. The newly formed Finnish government renamed the sea fortress Suomenlinna in 1918, literally Castle of Finland, rather than Viapori. In Swedish, however, it is still called Sveaborg. During the Winter War in 1939, the fortress was a base for the Finnish submarine fleet and after the Continuation War (1941–1944) only a few military units remained there. When the Coastal Artillery Regiment moved out in 1972 the sea fortress was turned over to civilian administration; only the Naval Academy remains there today.

Suomenlinna was added to UNESCO's World Heritage List in 1991 and is one of the most popular tourist attractions in Finland. It is also one of Helsinki's districts, with about 800 residents, and hosts various cultural institutions, museums, restaurants and so on. Military history and the sea have co-created the environment, which is continually changing. Some rare vegetation dates back to Russian times, when seeds arrived with the building materials and workers from the east. Some of the birds are relatively new arrivals, like the barnacle geese, which have begun to nest there during the last twenty years. They have not taken over the main islands as completely as they have occupied Harakka, the bird island, during the summer months.

Islands are easily conceived as meeting places, as suggested by geographer Doreen Massey (1994). According to her, places are processes; places can be understood not in opposition to an outside but through their particular links with that outside; places are full of internal conflicts about their past as well as their future; the specificity of a place is continually reproduced, from layers of different sets of linkages; the character of a place can only be constructed by linking that place to places beyond. Therefore, we need a global sense of the local, she insists – a global sense of place. (Massey 1994) The occasional fisher-men of earlier times, when the islands were only islets far out at sea, the Swedes beginning the fortifications, the Russian soldiers and officers continuing the fortifications, the Finnish military experimenting with explosives or training for combat, the prisoners of the civil war still haunting the barracks, the mate-rials washed ashore from ships passing by and later the various inhabitants of Helsinki and the visiting tourists finding an easy place to experience history and 'wild nature' close to the city centre, not to forget the artists, the environ-mentalists and ordinary families who live and work there today; all these and many more meet on those rocky islands and contribute to their specific sense of place. In this case it is easy to understand that there is no single identity and that place and community do not easily coincide. Over the years various communities have used the islands. Most of the inhabitants come and go like the migrating birds, including an extensive number of visitors from all over the world.

Artists have often found their way to Suomenlinna. There is the Ranta-kasarmi gallery run by Helsinki Artists' Association near the ferry harbour. Since 1968 there has been an open-air theatre in the Good Conscience ravelin on Susisaari island, in summer time. Before HIAP (Helsinki International Artist Programme) which is active in Suomenlinna today, there was NIFCA (Nordic Institute for Contemporary Art) until 2006. I remember performing in the Rantakasarmi gallery with the group Homo $ in 1984, in a piece called 'Empty Spaces'. We were hiding behind the vaults and sending toys and objects across the room to be the main performers before the girl band Joan Bennett Museo started playing behind the audience. More recently, in May 2011, I remember watching Tuuli Tubin perform her M.A. degree show in Live Art and Performance Studies, 'Beyond the Wind in Front of Me / A Space Ship Journey' on the southern shore, timing her actions with the passing giant ferry to Stockholm. Even more recently, in 2014-2016, Tomasz Szrama organized 'Tonight' – performance art events in Gallery Augusta on Suomenlinna. The events ran through the night, so the audience had to stay until the first morning ferry… I have described my experiments with a swing on two nights elsewhere (Arlander 2018). All these events took place on the main islands, not on the more 'hidden' Länsi-Mustasaari, the site of *On the Surface of Time*. Besides showing us another aspect of the well-known sea fortress, the performance allowed us to experience one of the main attractions on Suomenlinna, that is, walking along the cliffs, enjoying their soft, worn-out slopes; moving among the rocks, the reeds, the dry summer grass, and listening to the sound of the sea, with the view of Helsinki harbour as a backdrop, slowly sliding on the surface of time.

Annette Arlander // DA, artist, researcher and pedagogue, is currently Visiting Researcher at the Academy of Fine Arts, University of the Arts Helsinki. Until recently she was Professor in performance, art and theory at Stockholm University of the Arts. For artworks and publications: www.annettearlander.com.

References:

Arlander, Annette (2018): 'Process as Performance or Variations of Swinging', in Hetty Blades & Emma Meehan (eds.) *Performing Process: Sharing Dance and Choreographic Practice*. Bristol: Intellect Books, pp. 99-118.

Arlander, Annette (2012): 'Performing Time Through Place', in Riku Roihankorpi & Teemu Paavolainen (eds.) *SPACE–EVENT–AGENCY–EXPERIENCE*. Open Access E-Publication of the DREX Project. Centre for Practice as Research in Theatre, University of Tampere. http://hdl.handle.net/10138/37340

Empty Spaces (performance). Nordic Art Centre, Suomenlinna, Helsinki 1984.

Helsinki International Artist programme: https://www.hiap.fi/

Massey, Doreen (1994): *Space, Place and Gender*. Cambridge: Polity Press, pp. 146-156.

Swinging Tonight. Performance with projection at Tonight event, Suomenlinna 25.7.2014.

Tonight events: https://blacktonight.tumblr.com/

Tubin, Tuuli: 'Beyond the Wind in Front of Me': http://performanssi.com/beyond-the-wind-in-fron-of-me-a-space-ship-journey/

World Heritage Site Suomenlinna: https://www.suomenlinna.fi/en

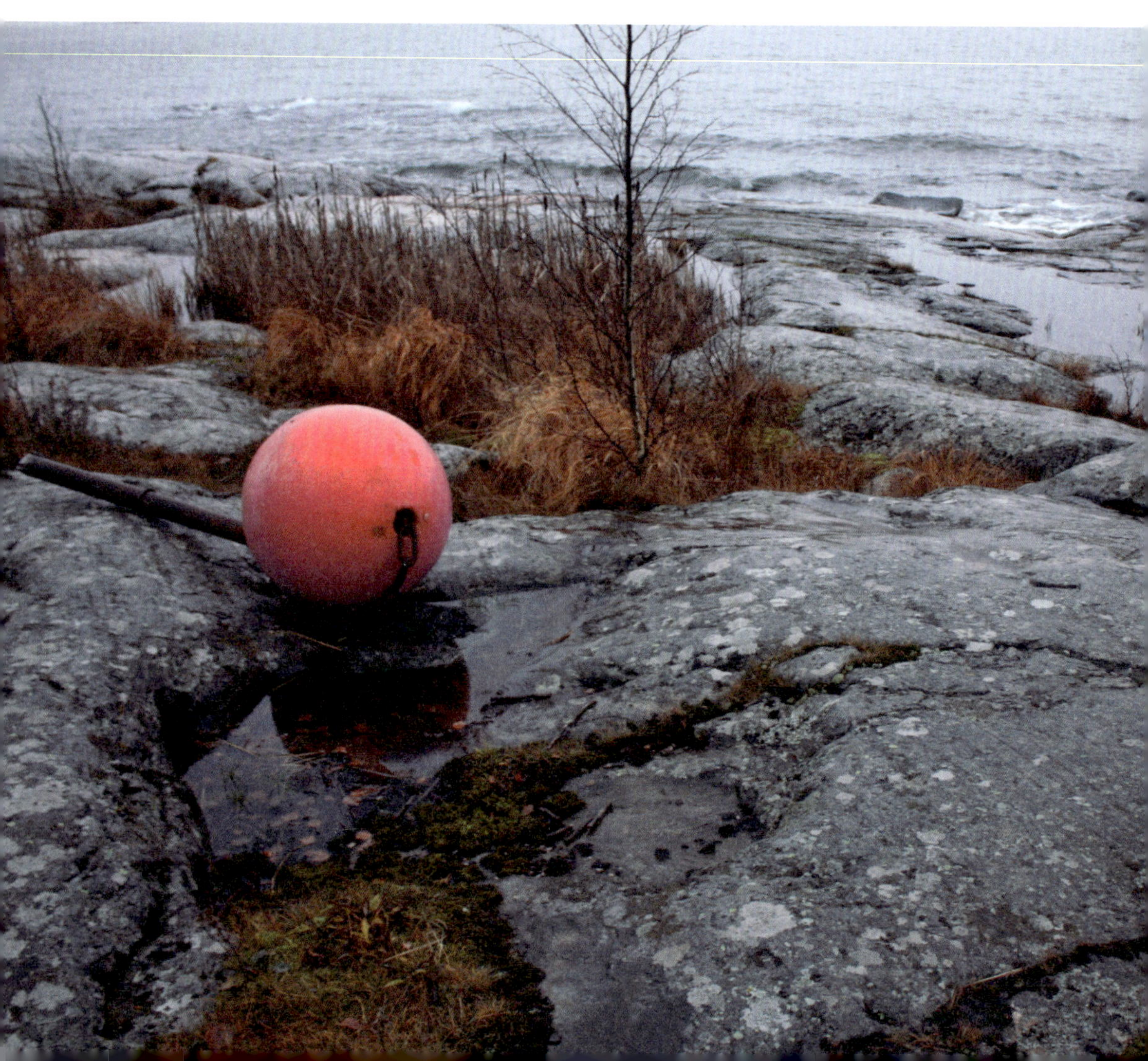

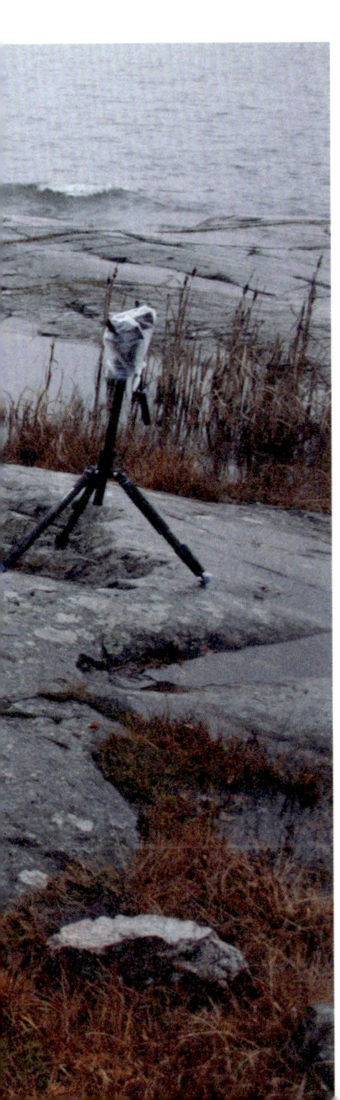

PRACTICE

I am with surface, with crust, with movement
underneath. I sink. Into the rock, meeting
its form as I come out with my elbow. I
see, feel, hear, taste, smell, sense winter
all around me, with its quietness and cold.
(11.02.2018)

Es ist stürmisch und warm, die Möwen sind
zerzaust. Ich habe fast ein fiebriges Gefühl,
einfach weil es überall so warm ist, und
dann wieder windkühl. Irgendwann muss es
doch regnen? Ich weiß es nicht.

It is stormy and warm, the seagulls are
tousled. I feel slightly feverish, just
because it is so hot everywhere and then
again wind-cool. Is it going to rain at some
point? I don't know.
(28.07.2018)

SUOMENLINNA
– Practising Movement

//Paula Kramer

I have been in movement and stillness on Länsi-Mustasaari (Länskäri) regularly between December 2016 and May 2019. 42 days, sometimes twice a day, especially in my final rehearsal period. It is a hot summer and I come early in the morning and late in the evening.

The work on the whole happens in a wave: a tentative and some-what unspecific beginning, a gradual intensification, a gathering of strength and momentum and then spreading out, trickling in, perco-lating slowly.

I walk some 25 minutes to site and once I have arrived roam around some more. At first I enter the site this way and that, moving here and there, testing, slowly becoming acquainted. The site is varied, where do I start today? Usually there is some kind of storyline, connective thread – where did I stop last time, where do I begin now? On the upper level or down below by the water? How is the site populated today, what is happening and where is the sun, the wind? I move in places that I don't recognize the next time I come, with the ice melting and everything changing, and everything unfamiliar still. Moving by a wall made of rock that I never return to. Many firsts.

I often find my way by lying on the rock. With my side, back, front I meet rock, lying down in surrender. Knees, arms, legs, torso – all arranged in their own way. Like this, I feel unmistaken. Gravity, surface, temperature. Immense (time)scales held in the rock, also in the wide sky above. Some noises around me, some animals, always. The city, sometimes more, sometimes less audible. The wind. The water. Ferries. Boats. Humans. But also: stillness. In the midst of all this, tuning into my body, sensing my form. Meeting and being met by the rock underneath. Held. Lying still and moving in lying. Just my lower legs moving, my arms sliding across the rock, making angled forms. Rolling, sometimes creeping.

My initial diary entries are interspersed with notes from seminars, meetings, conferences, telling me later that I did not yet have a dedicated movement journal. With time, the work intensifies; from September 2017 onwards becoming much more concrete and gathering impact, vitality. I am finding my way. Forms, weathers, colours, sounds, spacing, places – I return to something known, always new. I find buoy in the sea, pink and plump; buoy who becomes my companion, my significant other.

Routines emerge, they change but are recognisable still: walking, moving, filming, photographing (house and boat). I struggle with the filming in the beginning. I don't know the camera yet, setting everything up is time-consuming, the equipment is heavy. *The whole camera thing is a big hassle. It takes me a long time to set up and then I feel caught by the frame so easily. I don't see or feel beyond much. (26.05.2017)* The sound is often disrupted by the wind. What I need is an external mike with a windscreen. "Too laborious!" the mover in me exclaims. I am here to move and not to create video material!

Over time though, I befriend the camera as well as the video material. It happens during a first sharing in April 2017: I offer edited clips and invite the audience to accompany their viewing with drawing alongside. Fleetingly touching, holding, sketching, whatever it might be that touches them from what they see. I participate in this process and enjoy myself tremendously. Finally I dare to look at the video material closely. My hands have something to do and I can focus. Scrutinize, in a friendly way.

In August 2017 I spend an extended 'Day in the Gallery' at Uniarts Exhibition Laboratory with post-doc colleagues, again sharing this work through video. This time I project the uncut material, drawing alongside for hours. I leave the gallery very satisfied. Again I was able to look, able to see, able to sense and recap. And share with people who visit something from elsewhere, from that island there, from that winter now past.

From this experience and with the help of technicians working for the Fine Arts Academy (KUVA) I develop a format in which I can mix and overlay pre-recorded videos with live projections of materials and drawings on a table top in front of me, accompanied by speaking and occasionally also moving. Through this process I make peace with the camera on site. Whatever I record, it can be rough and raw. I now know that I will later mix and work further with it, sharing it in a live context rather than projecting a finalized film.

Yet I also feel liberated during my final rehearsal period in July and August 2018, a period I don't accompany with filming, a time in which I relish traversing space, attending to no-frame. In terms of intensity, this time forms the peak of the wave. I work in two longer stretches, during the second one I don't leave the island for nine days. I build and rebuild my score, entering deeply into the process of making.

I am immersed and the wave meets the shore. I share the work through workshop and performances; what has intensified flows out, spreads and ripples. I return to site three times after that, over the course of almost a year. Harvesting in November 2018, resting in January 2019, saying my farewell in May 2019. Autumn, Winter, Spring/Summer. Again I have time to move just for the sake of moving. Not preparing, not rehearsing, not performing, not documenting. Only moving. Digesting and saying farewell.

Seasons

I come to Helsinki in clusters, mostly once a month, spending a minimum of one day without leaving Suomenlinna. A day, or two, or three, for practice. This periodic being on site makes the seasons very strong. I come in icy months, in bare months, in green months. I come in the months with geese and I come in the months without geese. I come in the months with tourists, I come in the months without tourists. I move with the ice, move with the snow, move with the snow that once was. Move with bird song, move with birch leaves, move with the summer winds, move with the autumn storms.

Winter

The first season I meet is winter. Ice and rock, rock and ice. Small snowflakes and big ones, icy snow scratching over rock surfaces. The bright sunlight even brighter and also the total overcast, the heavy, heavy, endless grey. I am a guest of winter, not having to endure the lack of light for many months. I can fall in and out of this winter, totally enraptured by snow and the deep time of rock.

For now I sit here. Small flakes of snow blowing past me. I can hear the wind and the sea and some traffic from the mainland. My back is half touching black-red rock, multicoloured by a cover of moss and lichen. Before I get colder and stiller I will meet this moment, this place in movement, just a little bit. (15.01.2017)

Winter is also:

Cold, wet, grey – not so easy. Little bits of snow left, but on the whole it is not terrifyingly cold or wintery, rather it is damp. I like to look at the world, not so much move in it. I take quite some time to find my place to begin. A stone circle has been built – maybe a visitor, a resident, an artist. A black plastic bag on a small branch installation with German essential oil capsules inside. I am neither very satisfied nor very unhappy with my practice. The intertwined tree invites me, this time I respond, I am not sure if I have ever before? It is cosy in there, someone has installed a roof. For a while I am still, then my body softens and I can begin to dance (a little). I am quite satisfied to sit, witness, listen. (27.01.2018)

Winter has both – the total stillness, muffled sounds. Sea covered by ice. And also moveability – ice melting, dripping. The melting can come quickly. I once return to practice with urgency (rather than joining a seminar on the mainland) because the ice is beginning to talk, crackling under the surface. Ice shields moving on the water, small rivulets quickly emerging between enormous planes.

I, also, am sometimes more mobile and sometimes more still, in the winter. *How mobile I am, I feel when I see these icy rocks very still and the ice on the sea moving, ever so slightly. (11.02.2017)* I write this on a day just before the ice begins to melt, and movement re-emerges *with little swimming creatures moving under the ice, a swan flying by, a bit of sun. The world is waking up again. (13.02.2017)*

Other winter days speak ever more deeply of stillness and endless cold. Once I crouch, tightly huddled, by a slanted rock. Leaning my face towards ice, snow, rock. My head covered with hat and hood. Small, intertwined movements, a small package, me. I struggle to find my way in the beginning, but finally sink deep, deep into winter. I hear nothing, I see nothing. Just when I profoundly meet this endless depth and vastness of winter and rock, someone calls out to me. I am totally startled, looking up in alarm. I see a person, standing, waving. Friendly, both hands raised, calling from a distance. Further away than I had thought. Quickly I return to here, breathing out, also raising both arms, hands, waving. Yes, everything OK! Kiittos, thank you!

I want to continue, endlessly, but cold is creeping in and I have to admit that I'm not able to work further. Die schneegezuckerte Stille ist so wunderbar, ich will sie noch nicht ganz verlassen. Nie wieder wird die Welt genau so sich zeigen – einmalig, fragil, bemerkenswert so kommt mir alles vor. The snow-peppered silence is so particular, I don't want to leave it quite yet. Never again will the world show itself in quite the same way – unique, fragile, remarkable everything seems to me. (28.01.2018)

Spring

Summarized in one long quote from my movement diary, a day that I work without camera, this is the spring:

It feels like the snow has just melted, stepping on the old elephant's back. The dominant colours on the rocks are blueish green-greys, otherwise faded yellow-brown-white. Grey-blue the water and light blue the sky, with many white-grey clouds. It is sparkling and glittering and bright with the sun and the wind has ceased for a moment. Buoy is still here, rosy-pink and so man-made, nestled by the birch, just where I left her. Geese everywhere, mit langen Hälsen spähend und Gras knabbernd with long necks, prying, and nibbling grass, everywhere. I am happy to see that spring is here too!

I work a lot in lying, the perspective changes totally, drastically – sense of hearing, sense of seeing, sense of vulnerability, sense of scale.

I traverse quite some space, free without the framework of the camera.

Then I lie still on the rock, when I close my eyes something relaxes more, from there, maybe, one day I can move. The ducks arrive and now the swans are here. All in pairs, plump and fat. How do they decide where to go next? Who follows whom? Zwei Bachstelzen sind auch unterwegs, aber eher solistisch. Und leichtfüßig hüpfend. Two white wagtails are also out and about, following their own pathways, hopping light-footed. I stay, I sleep, I move in lying. I traverse backwards in animal height. In standing by the small rocks I move the small busy movements of the water and all the small and medium size rocks and boulders. Busy, standing, shaking. I then lie in the cleavage of a rock – it is totally relaxing. Nestled in. Supported by. Again I could lie forever. (21.04.2018)

Late Summer and Autumn

The total summer I experience during my final rehearsals, with heat and an unexpected number of sunbathers on the site, with a sailing regatta and hammocks. Suddenly I am sharing the site with several other humans, suddenly it is so hot that I choose the early morning and late evening to work in. A short period, which passes. The previous year, I spend the summer elsewhere, it is September when I return, late summer already, early autumn.

A journey. Lots of singing and sounding, moving, feeling totally disconnected. Then taking listening and receiving into my moving and sounding and doing and disconnect. And then slowly-slowly I become more transparent, available. I am still energetic, but also moving from. Satisfying! And then crawling. On my hands and feet. Backwards. A long journey. I don't know where I am going, but it feels great. I am going, going until I hit a border, the shore, the water. I turn, along the shoreline, continue and then there is a plate, a palm, a plateau, a rock-front-side – open to receive me and I see the sky in the clouds. (04.09.2017)

I find buoy on this day, and when I return to site in the afternoon, I pull her up to the shore, up on the rock, up on the large, grey slates. We move together for the first time, in the evening sun of September, the video material has quite a story line. Buoy comes with a long, heavy, rusty iron chain and a rusty iron rod, that may have kept her steady once, somewhere. The stories that emerge, then and over time, are full of Greek mythology. There is Sisyphus, Prometheus, Atlas – the heaviness of Sisyphus's boulder, the iron chains of Prometheus. The world as globe, as planet, is embodied in buoy. I carry her like Atlas, only in lying. Or have my shoulders, neck, next to her. And further: tales of a dead seaman, of slavery, of a prisoner once, somewhere. And also: sheer joy over such an object, here. Improbably large, improbably pink, improbably round. From now on we move together, here. Each time I return it's part of my arriving ritual to check if buoy is still around.

What a wild morning it was. So wild! So much wind, rain, cold, autumn, force. Jumping and saying and singing. And then finding buoy again, she was, is still there, I get almost a bit overexcited. I love you, I love you, I love you! I'm so happy you are here. Und insgesamt kracht mir die gesamte Kraft der Welt entgegen, mit mit all ihrer Liebe und ihrem Dasein, für uns alle. And on the whole the total force of the world is crashing towards me, with all its love and availability for every one of us. Thank you. (28.10.2017)

At some point I worry that buoy overshadows all the rockiness of this site. At other times I worry that she might vanish and never return. But over the course of my time working here, she remains. In the winter I let her rest, snow gathering on and around her. In the spring we re-enter moving together, alongside each other, in dialogue.

Moving Through, Moving On

When I come to say my farewell, I see buoy lying in a totally different place for the very first time. Rather than out by the rocks she is lying next to the pathway that cuts the site in half, divides the upper from the lower level. I am totally startled. Someone has moved buoy. Who? Why? My first impulse is to drag her back. But no. Apart from the fact that I am as round as buoy, carrying my second child and there is no way I could do this now, I also realize that buoy is now subjected to other hands, winds and forces. I let her go. Next time you go to Suomenlinna, do have a look for me if she is still around.

Coming from Berlin, from asphalt, trees and hours away from the nearest shore I am always slightly dazzled by the sheer beauty of Suomenlinna. The intensity of the seasons, the wide open sky, the presence of the sea, the air, the animals. The varied colours and the vastness of rock. Always there, allowing me to enter, to visit, to exit. Many wide open, smoothed and patterned rock surfaces, all of them different. Always with coarse ridges, changes in levels and materials, cracks and lines. The full impact of gravity and the vast availability of density, surface and tangible textures that I bodily sense and work with here. Impressed and impacted by the lines and cracks in the rock, the shifts in colour and material, the movement, the melting, the primeval forces and immense time span physically present here. Often the lines, cracks and crevices literally choreograph, make my movement. I directly follow the forms, lines and colours, they seep into me, my body translating their forms into dance, movement, gesture.

I can hear the city here, from afar, see it or not, depending which way I turn. I can sink deep and feel totally remote. Whilst people pass occasionally, I don't have to deal with being seen continuously. Questions about access are answered with generosity. I have to register my performances with the Governing Body of Suomenlinna and ask for permission, which is granted promptly. No fires allowed!

A vibrant quality of life is present here. The hare bones, the hare, a sense of seeing both ways, of sensing existential qualities of life, of death. *The border between life and death can be so thin. Transparent. I cannot see the other side. But I can feel this side change. (04.09.2017)*

I often reminisce on life, on Suomenlinna, as I do, in movement. Pondering, for example, what it might mean to witness this world, sometimes, rather than always plotting to add to it. A world rich in information, stimulation, offering, possibility. Overflowing, and here we are. Birds flying. Everything present. Thank you.

```
The skin, the crust, yes - the below, the
above, the earth, yes, the earth on me and
me on the earth, yes and the rock feels
so small suddenly.
(04.09.2017)

World, I bow to your forces. It is spring
happening all over again.
(18.05.2019)
```

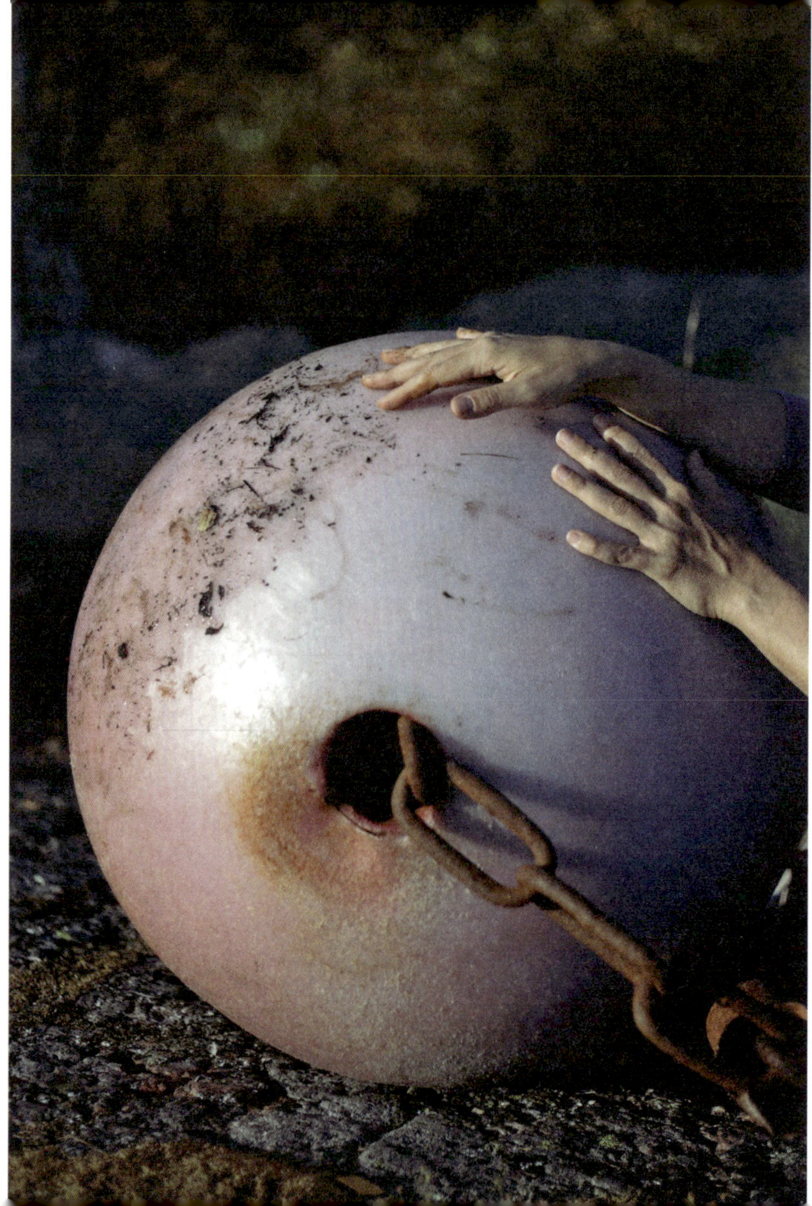

MEETING BUOY

Once upon a time
you arrived on a beach
by the sea
rocks and pebbles all around.

I pulled you up to meet with you
and over time we became friends.

Spending time together
over the course of a year.
Meeting and playing and testing
and trying and dancing and
resting.

And we performed together
on the surface of time.

In the winter I let you rest –

the world is still
the grass is still
the sea is ice.

Sometimes I move
and sometimes I am still also.

Will you be there next time I come?

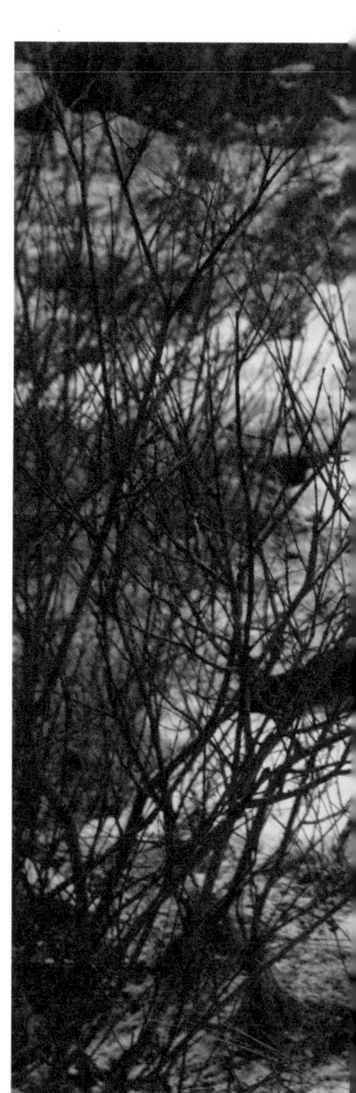

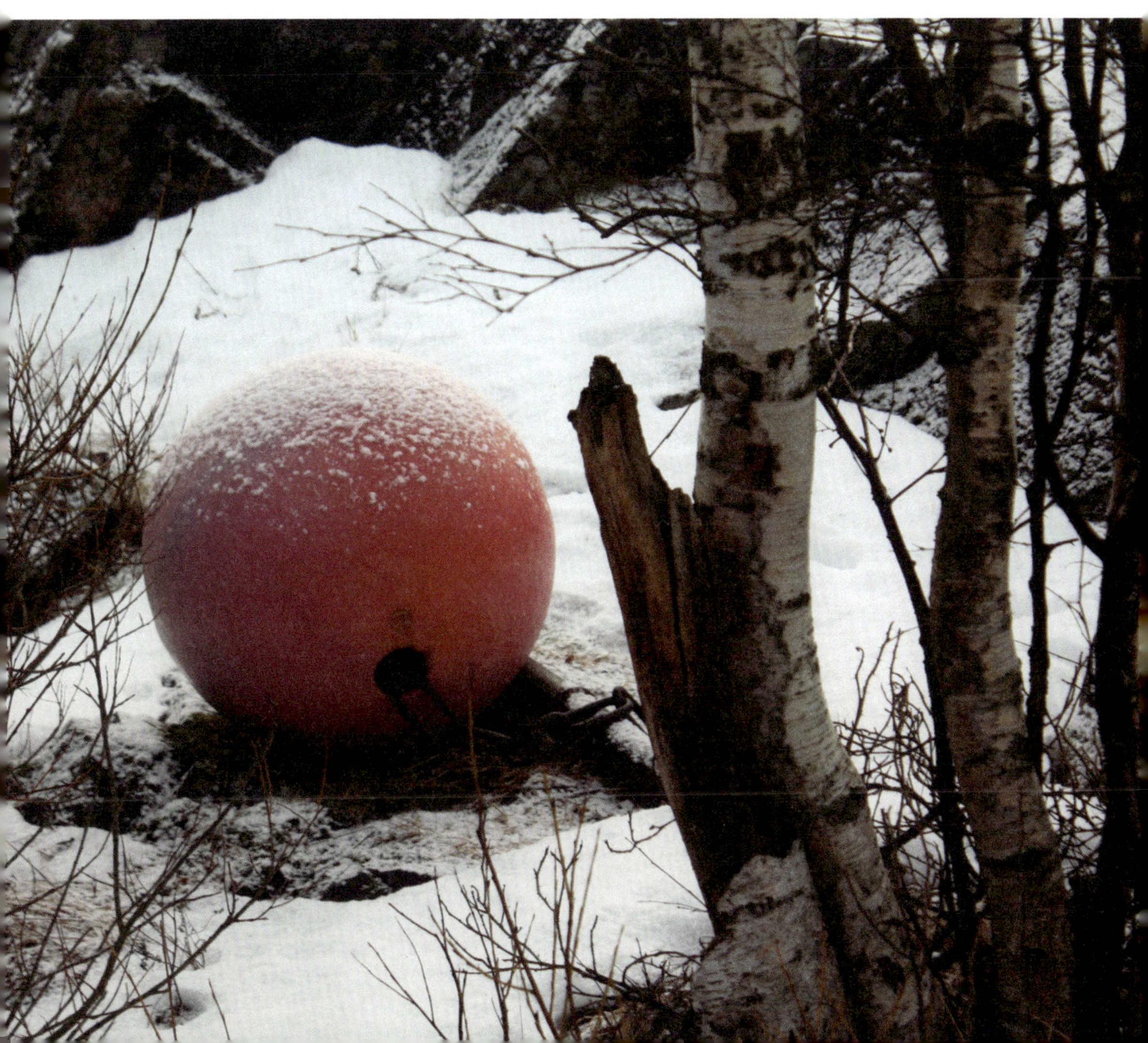

PERFORMANCE

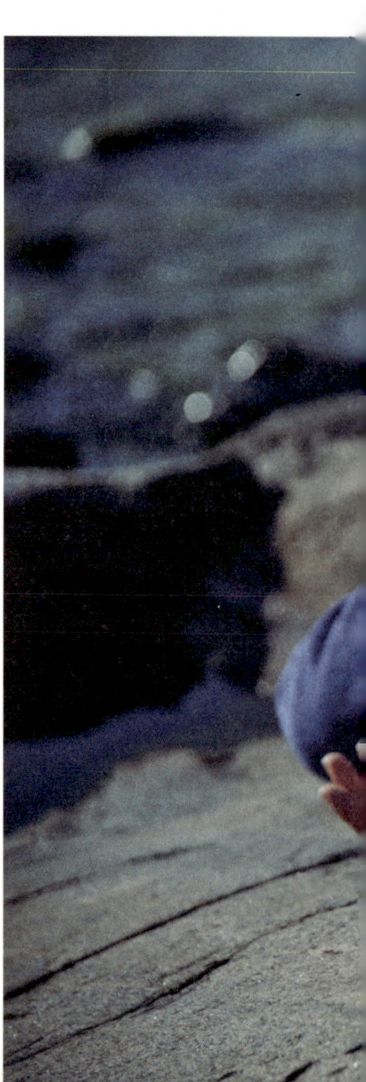

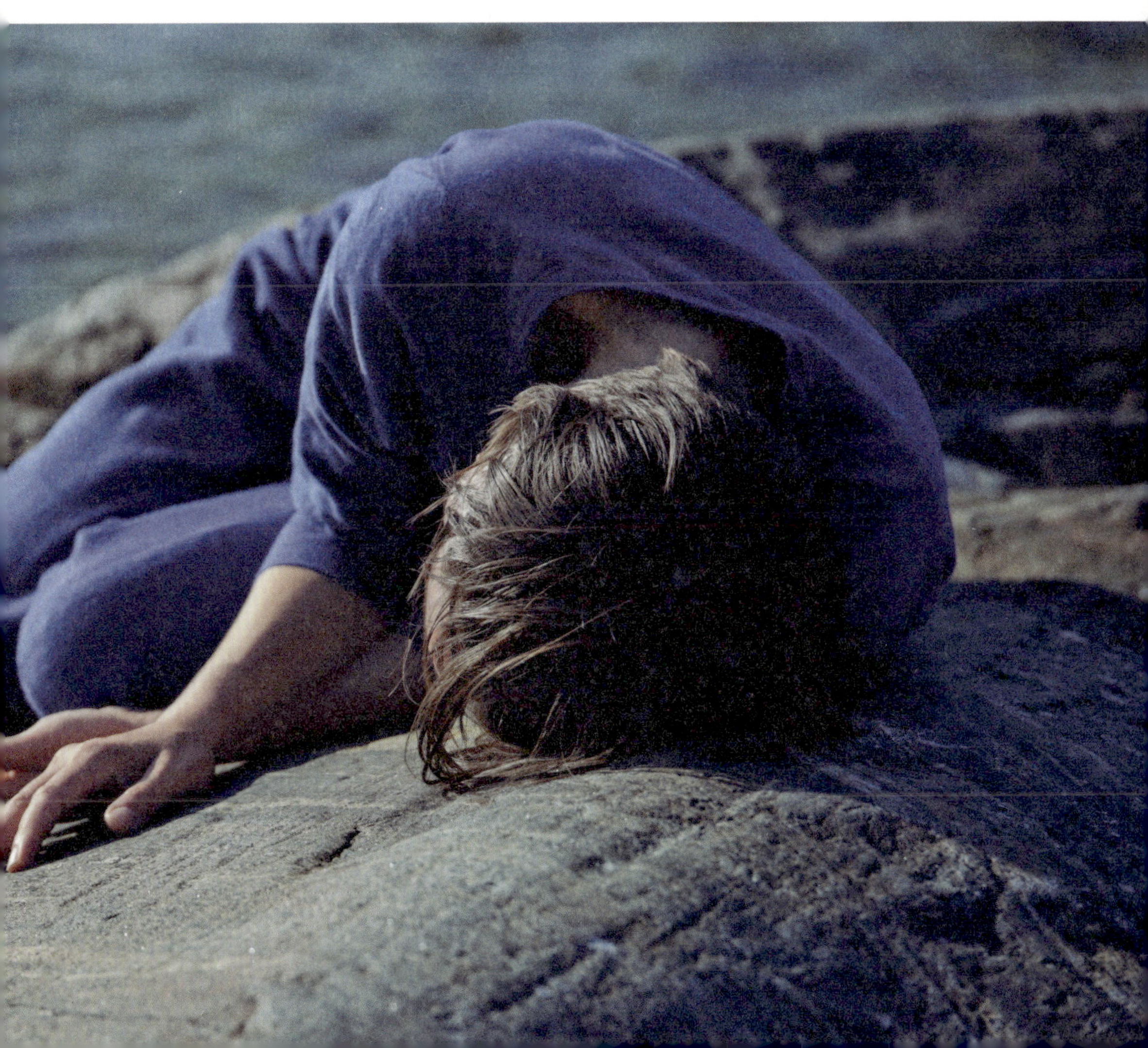

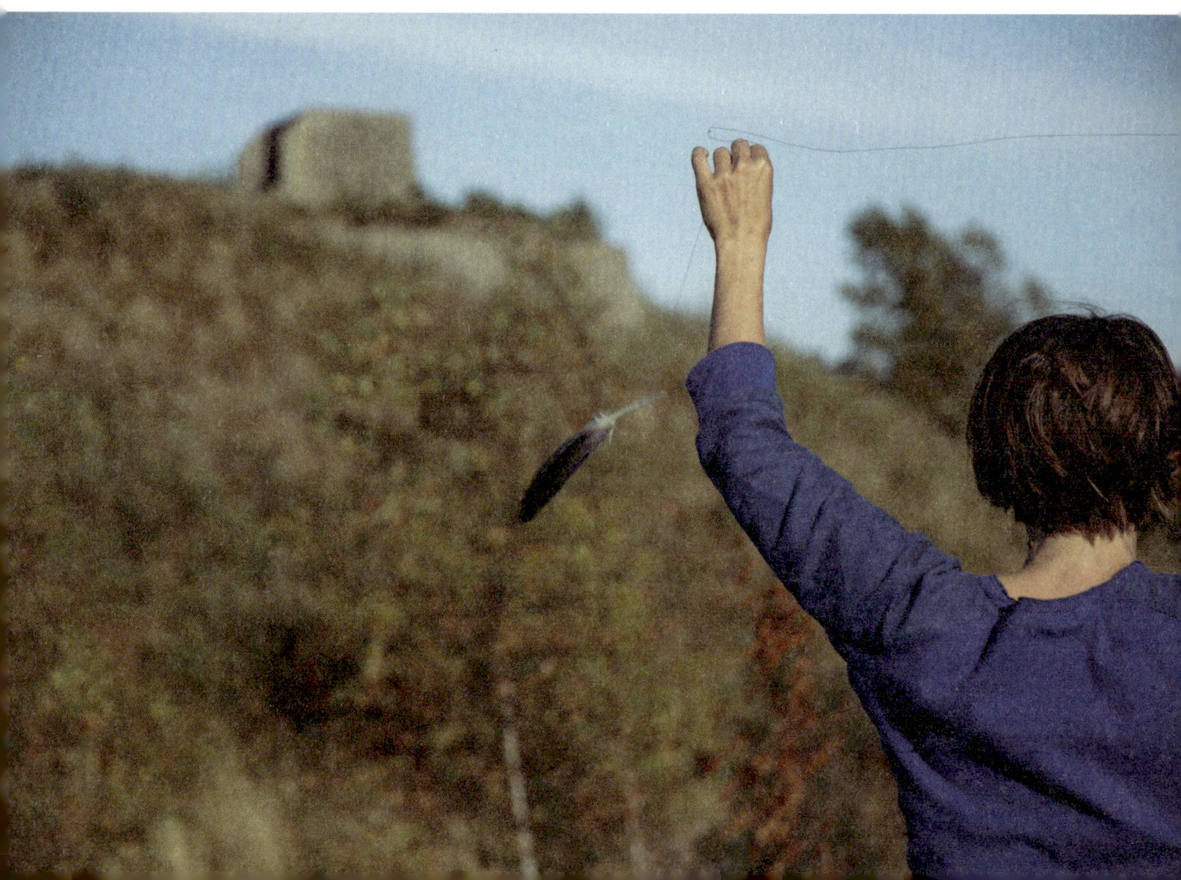

The Feather

//Annette Arlander

A feather swirling in the wind, tied with an invisible line to a dancer, like a miniature kite – this is the moment I most remember of that late summer afternoon on Länsi-Mustasaari. Why did I like the scene with the feather so much? In visual and dancerly terms the big buoy was a much more impressive partner, afforded more expressive bodily responses, and was more conducive of classic performance art actions. Perhaps it was not so much the feather, but the movement of the wind, the unexpected leaps and swirls of the feather that the wind generated, or the illusion of at least partial independence from human control it gave, that impressed me. It was as if the wind had been suddenly overtaken by some unexpected playfulness, producing this improvisatory lightness and joy. Or perhaps it was the change of focus away from the human body that inspired me; in this moment the dancer was only assisting in the duet of the feather and the wind. But why look for complicated reasons, perhaps I just loved the relationship of means and ends, how such a tiny gesture, like tying a feather at the end of a fishing line and flying it like a kite, could produce such hypnotic beauty, such an exciting and exhilarating effect.

Langsam werde ich mit dem Ort vertraut,
vertrauter, kann so etwas sehen, wie das
Stück mir entgegen kommt, habe schon ein paar
Markierungen gesetzt. Es ist nicht leicht
und wird doch schon kommen, in seiner Zeit.

I am slowly becoming more acquainted with the
site, more familiar, can already see how
the piece is slowly moving towards me, have
already placed a few markers. It is not easy
but will come in its own time.
(27.07.2018)

SUOMENLINNA
– On the Surface of Time

//Paula Kramer

I share the Suomenlinna research through a workshop and three evening performances in August 2018. A being-together on site, with dance. A making-of-contact with rock, body, sea, wind, weather, feather, buoy. A different framing and setting each day, golden-relaxed evening sun on the first, mysterious-near-rainy haze the second, strong-winds-post-rain on the last.

A different sense and movement quality emerges each time in response to the wider setting and the many details in play. A girl dancing alongside, a family crossing the performance in progress, a short dialogue in between, a different position, and gesture, and way of being in contact. Yet some markers remain the same, contributing to the mesh from which the performance is made.

I call the work 'On the Surface of Time'. A title I doubt occasionally, since I feel so often, and strongly, immersed deeply into time, into rock, into rock-time. Not on the surface. But the surface is there, always, is what holds, offers, invites, is what is visible and immediately present on site. I hatch the title whilst moving-rehearsing, accept it and make friends with it over time.

The Suomenlinna summer in 2018 is an intense process of crafting the performance score. I move, I write, I re-move, I re-write, I move again.

I re-turn to site again and again. Mornings, afternoons, evenings. For a period of nine days I don't leave the island at all, until the last performance is shared, until this deed is done.

It's not easy to take the score off my body, transposing what just happened in movement into words. Words that support me as I move through, with audience alongside. Words of just the right kind, poetic, open, supportive, adequate, accurate, space leaving, space giving. Words that carry me. Sometimes I move and I don't remember any of the specifics of my movements; what I did emerged and made sense, but the sequence, the exactness of whatever each movement was, what hands, arms, legs just did – disappears as the sequence subsides.

Of course I don't want to determine angles of limbs. This I cannot do, and really that would be a whole other kind of dance. But there is something I do need here, a story that whispers itself to me, sometimes from close by and sometimes from further away. A frame that gives me security when I lose it, as movement artist Helen Poynor reminds me in a mentoring conversation at the end of July.

My notes in July and August are continuous rewrites of the score. A repetition in variation of the same. In retrospect, it is fascinating to see how aspects, parts appear, how everything is forming itself. Clarity arises step by step. Something to trust in, in the future.

I find a Woman-in-the-Rock and a God-of-the-Rocks, I figure out pathways, starting positions, places in my body to initiate movement, when to take off and put on my shoes. There are always surprises: *The feather is behaving entirely unexpectedly, humming and turning like a propeller. It does not seem to work for the delicate pulling of strings as I had planned – but – it might be a good companion for crossing the 'upper stage' – I think so. (27.07.2018)*

Towards the end of my rehearsal period I find a paper slip from a German (!) fortune cookie: Jeden Tag einen Schritt weiter zu kommen kann auch ein schönes Ziel sein. Going one step further every day can also be a fine goal.

And so it was.

What follows is a notation of the performance score, handwritten and sketched on A3 paper after the public sharings. A first distillation. Edited again as I write the texts for this book.

Now this piece is here, to be repeated I suppose, or adapted, by myself, by anyone, by you.

THE SCORE

ONE – in the fold [shoes on]

I begin in the fold. Lying on my back. Listening. Opening towards sounds. On a small island of rock, cradled by the Baltic Sea. There are winds, birds, boats, waves, aeroplanes, humans, rocks, shrubs, grasses, trees, sky.

Here I begin. Rock beneath, sky above, slanted fold on both sides. Wrapped in deep time, time of rocks, thousands of millions of years. Head inland, feet towards the sea. When my head touches a small ledge in the rock I know I am in place.

Sometimes there is water in the fold. My left leg can rest slightly bent and raised on an uneven ridge. Sometimes one hand is placed on my torso and an arm gestures outwards, resting on the rock. But not always. Sometimes my eyes are closed when I begin.

I hear the waves, the water, all sounds. I can briefly zoom into this feeling of lying and listening, all alone, on a small island of rock, somewhere in a wide open sea. This is a good place for me to start.

Movement arises from slight diagonal movements in my sacrum. Distal end of my left arm moves in relationship. The sacrum movements are essential, places of detail can join, follow or lead – hand, forearm, arm. Still in lying I turn over my right shoulder. I can spend time in the fold, sideways, seeing the mountainous landscape around me (the sides of the fold appear like mountains from this lying position).

Eventually I turn again over my right shoulder and face downwards. I come up to animal height, exploring the rock with my hands, knees, feet, most often changing direction, eventually my head points to the sea, my feet inland. Here I learn to speak rockish. I say this to myself and move in response. Learning to speak rockish, I learn to speak rockish. I see the lines in the rock, the different colours and shapes, small cracks and ledges, larger features and forms.

Eventually I rise to standing, facing inland – towards the audience in a way. In my learning to speak rockish I either arrive there or otherwise walk or balance over ledge and slope to a specific standing position, my feet seeking to find good grip on the slanted surface. In the evening my shadow falls into the figure of a woman I discern in the rock. In the lines of the rock I see a woman standing, one arm horizontally out, one arm angled towards the sky. Sometimes we mirror each other.

From this mirroring form there are many variations. I am the Woman-in-the-Rock and move as her, she is my mirror and I am hers. I move in response to the lines in the rock, also the wider cracks. I both receive and greet the audience and open the space. This can also happen in sitting, but at least once turning wide open, once around my axis if possible, my arm(s), upper body and gaze opening the space, for me, for the audience, for the moment. It sometimes feels a little bit like opening a door. And sometimes also opening towards the sky, but only if it happens, if it's easy. I try not to force this.

I then take a few steps and kneel down, lie down, come down to the God-of-the-Rocks. A larger-than-human body lying in the rock, head towards the sea, feet inland. Big upper body, head, shoulders, arms. The outline vaguely reminds me of the Sphinx of

Giza. But then – long legs, or a long lower body. More human like. A big, strong figure facing the sky. Please receive me, I whisper, please, receive me.

I have purposefully not set anything further in this section. I practise surrender here. Please receive me, from here I move. Maybe I crawl around in what might be head and shoulders/arms of this God. Often filled with water. Always some. I might end up sliding down a slight slope, or finding my head or hand wet with water, or finding myself in an unexpected form. Physically I am in very low animal, close to the rock, close to the ground, close to the God, in surrender.

Sometimes I end this section crouched on the God-of-the-Rocks, often facing downwards. Always with the inner words: "Nothing of what you just saw ever happened, nothing ever happened here. Nothing of what you just saw ever happened, nothing ever happened here."

The section as a whole can be longer or shorter. After ending I pause a while in stillness. Then rise from the rock, turn to the audience, see what I see and say: "Let's go to the second site."

TWO – by the weapon [bare feet]

After arriving on the site I put down my backpack and take off my shoes.

I begin by the weapon. It is in my background, pointing towards the sky. You can see it or not, depending on how you are positioned towards me. It remains difficult throughout to find a fitting starting position here. For a long time I began with lying on my back, in a slight dent or hollow. Perpendicular, in a way, to the gun, the weapon. Left leg bent with my foot on the ground, right leg stretched out.

At some point I felt irritated by this position because it seems to resemble the starting position in the fold too closely. Two performances (I think) I begin here in standing, the third one in half kneeling. For sure I always face sideways to the weapon, weapon to my right, open rock surface to my left.

In standing I once note that a feeling of shooting out through my head is a possible starting point. Not always. In any case I begin with shooting, somehow. Gathering the quality of cutting through the sky, dividing and conquering (divide et impera) – I remember this expression when noting down the score in my notebook. Divide et impera.

On site I have an inner dialogue of: I cut, I cut through you. I divide the sky, I master / oppress and dominate you, you world, you humans, you everything. I shoot, I cut, I destroy. With very linear gestures all throughout my body, clear lines, clear angles. Clear lines of cutting, here, here and here.

On the whole I distil five, then six, qualities to draw on, to develop, to build.

1 CUTTING
SHOOTING
DIVIDING
LINEAR
GUN

2 RESISTING
REVOLTING
PROTESTING
YOU WILL NOT
GET ME
FIST and gesture
of PROTEST
THROUGHOUT
MY BODY
DEMANDING
JUSTICE
drawing energy and
support from the rock
learning from the rock
making use of rock quality

3 DYING
HELPLESS
CORPSE
DEATH
LIMP
GIVING UP
   CRYING
CAPITULATION
    in the face
of war, weapons
and injustice
    in this world
    I GIVE UP
open hands
WHITE flag

4 THE FACE
OF THE
EARTH ON
WHICH
ALL HAPPENS
AND WHICH
COULD NOT
CARE LESS

5 IF NOTHING
ELSE WE
HAVE OUR
FEET
to walk
away
to CHANGE

6 BEING INSIDE
THE MACHINE
   THE WEAPON
THE APPARATUS
   this coiled turmoil
unknown disorder
POSITION not metaphorically
but literally
BEING INSIDE
THE MACHINE
(sometimes I have this in my body
alongside the clearly visible linearity of 1)

I begin with quality one, if possible. Clear, clear, clear. Then quality two can join and counter, I will NOT give up, I will not give in, I will not let you (war, weapons industry, injustice) get me, get us, get anyone. This begins by turning towards the rock, seeking quality of rock in my body, strength, inspiration, support; fist in the air. It depends a little on me and my dialogue with the audience – how dramatic, explicit, I allow this to get. In between, or as a third, capitulation enters. I give up. I show both empty hands, here. I hold nothing. I am not shooting and I am not protesting any more.

There is a way of sequencing, alternating these qualities in my body. I can return to: shooting, protesting, capitulation and so on. Sometimes two qualities present themselves at the same time. (One hand, arm in protest, one capitulating). After a few, or only one, cycle(s) of 1 – 2 – 3, I introduce 4: all this happens on the face of this earth, on the face of this earth, that lives on, that remains, that continues onwards, that has been here, these rocks, for 1.8-1.9 billion years and that will continue to be here when humans are no longer present.

And then I might cycle again, including all four, 1 – 2 – 3 – 4 – 1 – 3 – 2 – 4, and so on, any order, as it arises, as becomes possible, available. Sometimes quality 6 enters: I am also inside the machine that is shooting. There is a quality of material complexity, interiority alongside the clearly angled cutting.

The only thing set is that I begin with the shooting and I counter with resistance. From there on I can see what shows itself, what becomes available.

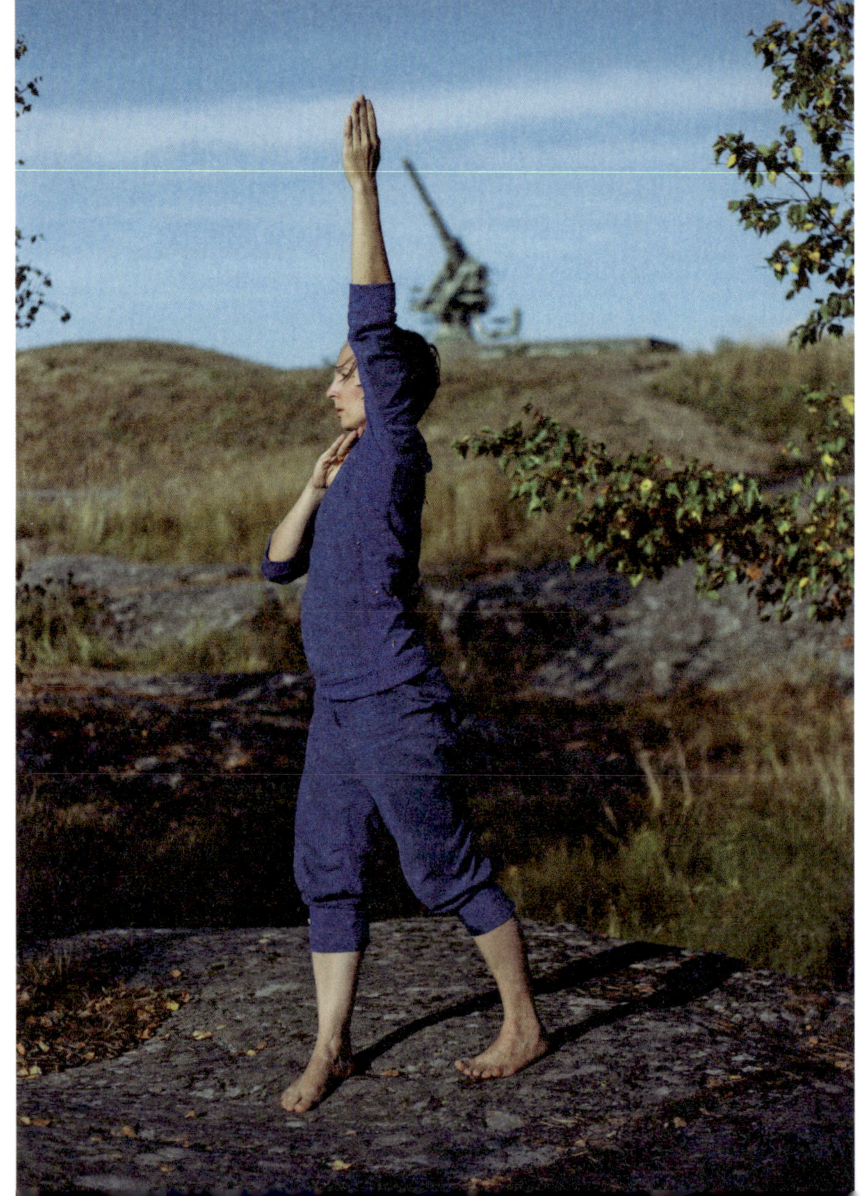

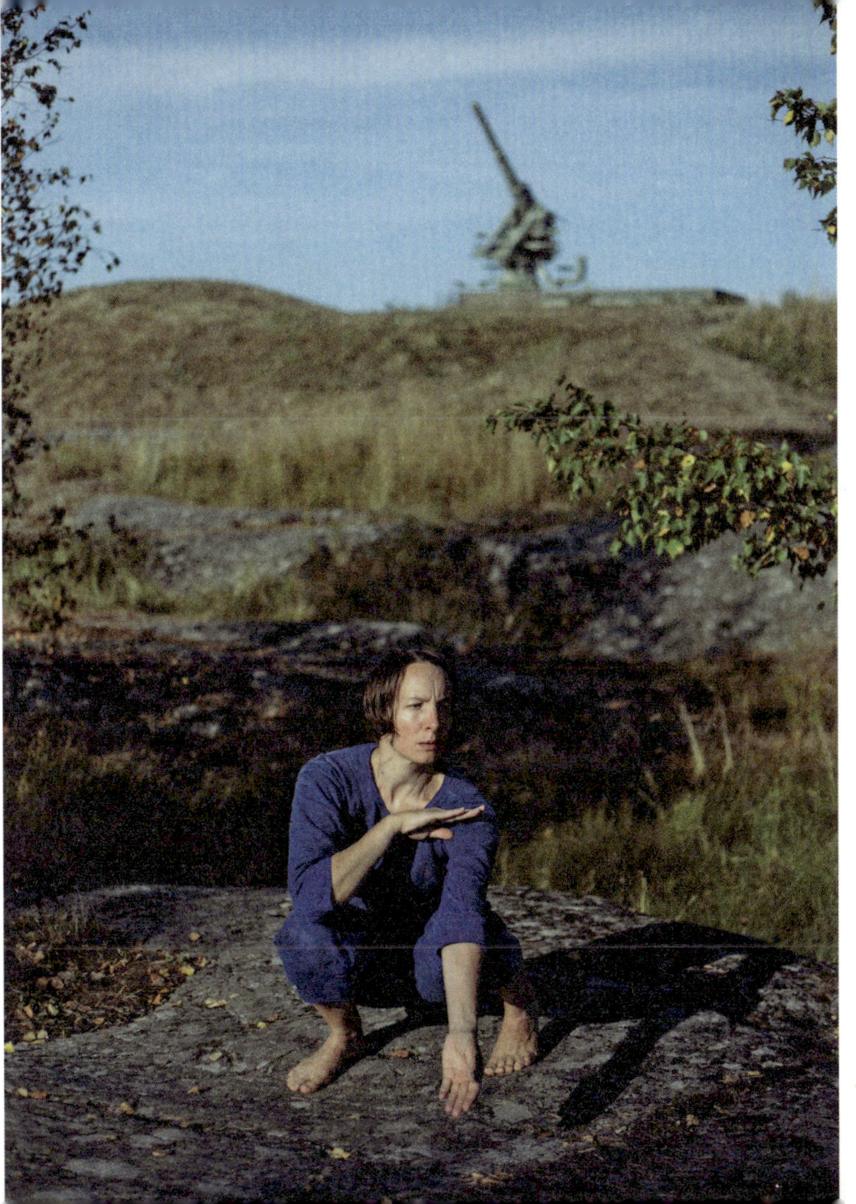

I might end crouched down in protest, frustration or despair, maybe. Over time I realize (I think this came through performing or maybe just before) that there is a way out. I can 'remember my feet' (Helen Poynor's words) and my ability to walk, to walk out, to change position. From then on quality 5 often becomes my end to this section.

I can / we can remember our feet, I can / we can remember that we can walk (out), I can / we can remember that there is a way. This came as a satisfying addition for me, a way to tune down the high emotionality, a way to return to here, now, this site. And a gesture, a movement that allowed for a sense of possibility. If available.

THREE – the feather [bare feet]

I bend down and pick up a prepared feather. There is a hole in the moss already where I insert the feather each time. I pick up the feather and hold it in my hollow hand. Or by its quill. Quite lightly, so the wind can move it. I look at the feather, observing how it is moved by the wind.

During my first rehearsal period many goose feathers are scattered here, and also on all the other Suomenlinna islands. I begin to collect them, they are so obviously around. And I begin to see an inner image of me standing on the edge of the upper site, holding a string with a flying feather attached to it. Like a kite. When I first play with feather and string, this does not work at all.

The strung feather surprises me, beginning to spin and sound like a loud propeller as soon as I release it into the wind, holding onto the string. Totally unexpected. It is fun, playful, and so different from what I had imagined. I go through several possibilities with the feather. One includes stroking the rock with the feather and also myself, the back of my head especially. The different sounds are intriguing – feather over rock, over moss, over lichen, over skin, hair, etc. – but especially feather on my body seems to resemble shamanic cleansing rituals and I feel not entitled and not clear enough in my intention with that. So this falls away again.

In performance I hold the feather for a while, loosely, with movement potential, but still in my hands, casually. Until in standing or kneeling I unwind its thread and let it fly – first the thread in the air, then placing the feather on the rock. I pull the feather over the rock, as I am walking to the edge where I will move next. It gets caught occasionally and ever so slightly by the coarse surface of the rock. Lichens, mosses, cracks, small ledges make it stop, jump, move unevenly (very slight all this).

And then I can lift it and the wind begins to play with it. And before it gets too much, before it begins to spin drastically and the thread gets all wound up, I lower it again. So there begins a game of lifting and lowering and me dancing and turning with it. Positioning the feather also in front of my torso (flying), by my side, overhead – many possibilities. Feather lying and feather flying I think now and remember my movement teacher Prapto. I do this until I reach the ledge where I continue. Here I let the feather go and fly towards the audience. On the first night I take the thread off (something I had tried only once, the day before). The next two nights I let the feather fly still tied to the thread and this happens more seamlessly.

On the first night the feather falls into the small tree right in front of me, no big flight. But then it drops one branch lower when I move down in a fitting synchronicity. On the second night an audience member picks up the feather with the thread and continues to play with it, someone else continuing with this game as we walk down to the next site later on.

FOUR – mountain range [bare feet]

Once, there was a mountain range and it was right here, right here. High and tall, tall and high.

I stand on a small, rounded rock 'stage', slightly elevated. There is a small, dry tree quite close to me. Sally (as first peer witness) had seen my moving there as a duet with this tree. She had seen me seed-like.

For me the movement begins in dialogue with the big grassy elephant backs that I can see from here. Some old storage spaces underneath them, probably. One, two that I can see well. My back rounds in relationship to them, round and arched also. I become heavy, heavy rock, connected through my feet and legs, strong in my back. Later, I also connect, and sometimes this is easier, with the big, big mountain range that once was here. Of which we are now at the foot, at the absolute bottom after 1.8-1.9 billion (1,800 to 1,900 million!) years.

I can feel the mountain range clearly, I can stand right in it. My arms pointing downwards, long arms, slightly elevated and clear open hands, fingers outstretched. I am like an umbrella, I don't know why I say that, like a triangle, maybe, and there is just the right amount of tension to become a mountain, to be mountain, this mountain that once was.

My hands are strong and corresponding, my arms and then the whole body give form, and then the elephant backs are also there and the small tree and the seed forms that Sally once saw and then of course – the wide open.

The wide open, spectacular background, all is wonderfully visible from here. The sea, the sky, the trees, the drop down towards the sea – everything and all of it. So to this I open also, turning towards the sea at some point, reaching into the sky if possible and adequate. Showing, and telling of, this whole beautiful stage, site, place, world. Sometimes this can feel too grand and heroic. But if it gets too much, too far out, I can always return and slip into the big, big mountain range that once was here, and move within it, which I find completely satisfying.

I then close, say which way we are going, get my bag and we scramble downwards towards the third and last site.

FIVE – meeting buoy [shoes on]

I sit down to put on my shoes and get up to sit next to buoy. Leisurely, friendly, chatting. Sometimes I really whisper a few words. Hello friend, here we are again, you and I. I sit with my knees drawn up, my elbows resting on my knees, my chin sometimes resting in one or both hands. My forearms then moving, again distal movement of the arms is a point of beginning here. I sit right next to buoy before I begin any of this, just her and I and looking out, out to sea. Receiving the evening sky as it is today, wide open, always. We are about the same height, buoy and I, and we sit here, next to each other, chatting.

I am a human among other humans, I see where the audience members position themselves, and how. I see their colours, their clothing. Those, at least, who position themselves so that I can see them. I chat, and I look out, and I am here. My forearms and hands gesture. It is in some way as if I am telling a story. Yes. And there is this and that, the people, the sunlight, the mist, the sea. My head sometimes rests on my fist, or palm and moving through such points of contact, my head, neck, forearms, hands continue their little talking dance of changing gestures.

I then transition to leaning into buoy, maybe with my side, my cheek especially important, at least once I touch buoy with my cheek, feel the temperature, meet skin to skin, surrender to the touch, briefly. So after I tell buoy with my gesturing what is going on and I also tell the world that I'm sitting here with buoy, I touch and I surrender and I meet buoy as world, as globe, as planet.

She changes from my size to the size of the earth. This is where it's all happening, I think and might say to myself – here we are on the face of the earth. I might push buoy a bit with the side of my body, see how and where we roll, she rolls. Once, with Sally witnessing, we roll together, downhill; I am in front, buoy follows me. But in the performances it's more the other way around – I push buoy a little with my side, in animal height or crouching or something like that. And cheek, and side and somehow small, crouching, pushing. And then I sometimes roll up onto buoy, the earth, opening towards the sky. Earth on earth, globe on globe, here we are. And I roll back over.

Then begins the pushing and pulling phase. Sometimes pushing buoy like an animal would, a dog maybe, or a pig. Pushing buoy forward, but then also sometimes crawling on all fours in front of buoy and dragging her behind with one hand.

When Sally was here I gathered the chain in my arms, cradling an umbilical cord, and pulled buoy on it, looking at her, or sideways. Once in the three performances this comes back, but the main gesture, sometimes also directly after meeting buoy as globe, as earth, is me standing and pulling buoy behind me. My hands raised over my head, elbows folded, hands behind my neck. In this way I can anchor well and have good leverage.

And with all my might I pull buoy – down and up and across the rock face, towards the sea, towards the sea. Towards where you came from, towards where I once found you, one year ago now … I pulled you up in the same way then, it was the only way I could manage to move you up and away from the water.

What this part means to me and what I say to myself is: "Everything that happens here is real. Everything that happens here, in this performance, is real."

And I pull and I pull and when quite close to the edge of the sea I let buoy settle and drop the chain and leave buoy lying there. I move one, two steps away and also lie down, usually facing buoy, noticing for a short moment how we both lie, there, on the rock. I tend to lie with my head facing inland and my feet towards the sea.

Like this we are lying, facing each other.

Now that I write this it feels like I could have lain there for a little longer, to really notice how this feels, but I don't think in the performances I ever did this. It is more a moment in transit, a here we both lie now, on the open rock face close to the sea, and then I say goodbye in turning-turning.

I turn and I turn and I roll slowly away from buoy, into the next part and towards the end.

SIX – ending phase [shoes on]

I roll, and after a few turns notice how the bond with buoy dissolves. I look at her a few, two or three times, and then shift my attention away, cutting the bond, returning to rock. Maybe my rolling in relationship to buoy is still a bit softer, my body more bent, uneven, more human in a way. In this very human gesture of departing and this feeling of separation, there is a sorrow of leaving, of saying goodbye.

Then I turn to something new, towards the great big slate of rock that is so smooth, so polished, so soft, almost shiny, sometimes. The buoy part ends and the ending begins when my attention has left buoy and turned to rock, at the very latest when I approach 'the gap'. A crack opening between two kinds of rock – not huge, but it's an obstacle to cross for a rolling person. Two kinds of rock meet and break apart here, and in my inner attention one section ends and another one begins.

I roll and I feel the rock. I love this rolling. It is clear and easy, it is full contact with materiality, I am relieved to not be in human-dancerly-upright-standing-on-my-two-feet-responsibility. I roll for a while and then, the end has never been totally clear or easy. This could change, were I to do it again, but maybe this is also its nature and it will always be like that, no matter how refined.

I roll and I feel the rock. This soft, vast, smooth surface. It is such an elegant rock, this one, and I know it well. I roll and cross distance and about 2/3rds of the way across my legs tend to come up when I'm on my back and then I slowly come up to standing, passing through animal height. A point of orientation then are the many lines and cracks in the rock, going in many directions, so clear and dark, guiding my arms and my body. Here again a sense of moving within and against an impressive site and background, my body a point of connection.

Connecting up and down, land and sea, sky and rock, diagonals in my arms and elbows. Standing, yes, here, yes. The trees quite far away over there, the clouds, the boats, also. Movements of past sections can reappear, for example the linearity of the gun.

At least once in this section I try to stand so that I only see sky. My hands point out in a strange way and I look up, up and then over. My chest and arms face the sky and then I sometimes bring my gaze down, towards the rock. I also turn towards the sea and I see where people are placed, dotted all around. Once someone is sitting clearly outlined on a big rock in the sea quite far away and another person surprises me by sitting behind where the rock drops towards the sea, in the water, almost.

I tell the story of this site, turning in all directions. The trees, the sea, the rocks, the sky, the birds and us humans, all here, now. In the first performance I end standing quite strong and tall, but feel a sense of separation in relationship to the audience. So in the second run I sit down like all or many of the audience members and become one of them before I say thank you and end.

I don't remember how I did it in round three, but I think many were standing (it was windy and cold) and I ended as audience, standing. I enjoy this moment of performance energy dropping and 'becoming normal' again. Just human, me. After the thank you, and each time a bit awkward, I say "The end" or "This is it" or something like that. There's a better solution for this moment still, something that is clear, but not awkward.

On the whole, what remains is a sense of spaciousness and grati-
tude. To work on Länskäri in intense relationship to rock, to sky, to
tree, to sea, was something I could never have foreseen. And yet it
happened, it took place, and maybe one day, it will take place again.

It is all a matter of getting my head back
on my body. One tool is to touch my head.
Another to imagine relaxing the skin around
my brain - if I am able to do that, that
really helps.
(17.08.2018)

As I insert myself into the rock ledge, my
starting place, I look up and see a rainbow
directly above me. Just like that, straight
above. A small rainbow in a cloud. Something
I have never seen before.
(13.08.2018)

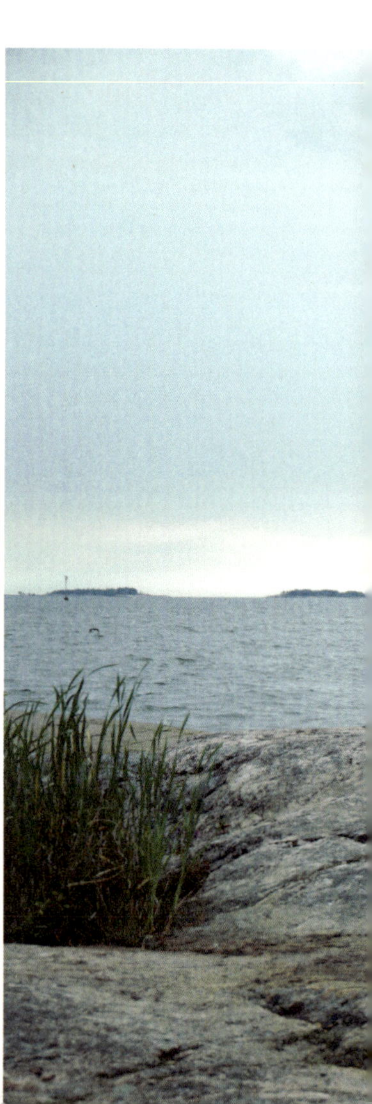

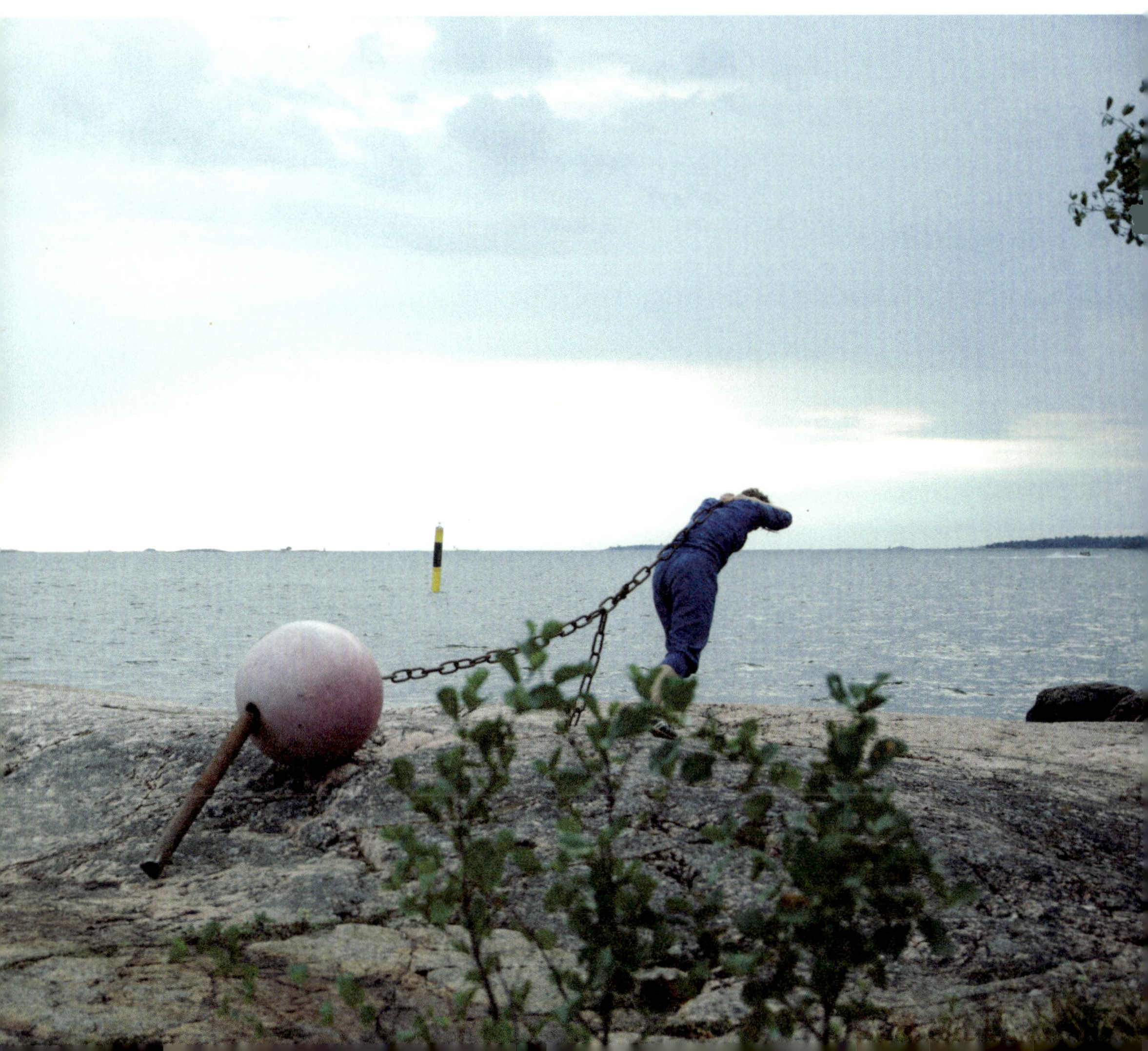

Placement Upon the Surface of Time

// Kira O'Reilly

I

Returning to Suomenlinna on the vernal equinox of 2019 I retrace my steps to the sites of the performance, bringing forward in my mind the shape and feel of the walk from the harbour. Alone and not in the congregation of audience this time, or perhaps not strictly alone given the extended company of the wind, lichens, swans, rocks, vegetation and sea.

The sea agitates in windy ripples and with it the rocks, released from the entirety of their stasis, appear to almost perceptibly swell. The round buoy on the rocks is faded and weathered to a dusty pink, anchored into *stonetime* with a rusting of metal chain. Multiple temporalities stretch and nestle themselves into intimate relations and alignments across 'The Surface of Time'.

II

The play of the August wind causes clouds to scutter across the skies, yachts' sails to file and glide, and soaring birds to circle.

The previous week we had talked about the wind: *I do not like the wind*, she said; *neither do I*, I chimed. On the deck during the ferry journey out to the island my long, uncut hair whips itself around my face in flustery movements. I secure it with a plastic hair accessory.

The sea is choppy, small Baltic waves (they never get big) motionful on the rocky edges where the rocks have absorbed heat all summer; now they are lazy with it, smooth, parched dry and massive. Rock pools' surfaces are scattered with small leaves from the nearby birches, ants follow complex pathways, small mossy crevices are alive with clouds of tiny midges as if moving in Brownian motion[1] made visible only by the sunshine catching their minuscule bodies.

As audience, our movement in relation to one another is that of a careful act of flocking. Our bodies cast long and curious shadows and I am careful that my mine, elongated by the low lying August sun behind me, does not touch her. The golden sun drenches the rocks and each pool ripples, birds soar and we sit, unmoving and some of us find smaller positions behind rocks out of the wind from which to peer at the performance.

Rhythms and phenomena in differing velocities phase into precise movements of connection before dissipating. In one sequence she rises and turns as a yacht, whose sails the wind has filled, moves across the middle distance of sea, seemingly in tandem with her rotation. The moment dissolves and transitions to...

A young girl from the island's kindergarten becomes literally moved to dance. Her body like mine, *re*-cognising; or maybe not – perhaps she is finding these movements and shapes for the first time. She grasps not only the transition of shapes but the actual forms, the light tensions of limbs that facilitate delicate yet definitive arrangements. The arms uplifted and bent at the elbows, the torso held so specifically, performing the massive mountain range that once was where we are.

A feather dances madly in the wind like a whirligig.

III

There is an assuredness and articulacy in the fluency of movement. She knows what she is doing; there is mastery there, accomplishment. She reveals knowledge as she unfolds and discovers it before us, yet this is not a finished

1. Brownian motion or Brownian movement named after the Scottish botanist Robert Brown (1773-1858), is the random and continuous motion of small particles within a gas or liquid medium.

endeavour. As she places weight on the rock, the rock places weight upon her and there is a confiding of reciprocity in the assured sensibilities of the movements. Her certainty of placement is in knowing exactly how the rest of the body will turn when the leg is moved across, understanding the origin of the movement, its interior and exterior provenance – where is it? A thought, an impulse, the wind, the stone, the water, the moss... what we witness is the performance of that re-search imbued with August sunlit clarity.

It is not improvisation, we say to one another on the ferry back to the mainland.

The movement is sustained – like a wave, he says.

I imagine it ebb – and thus making time for, as he says – reflection and response, allowing the movement to return – to flow, and then – to flow again.

Kira O'Reilly // is an Irish visual artist based in Helsinki; her practice, both wilfully interdisciplinary and entirely undisciplined, employs performance, installation, biotechnical practices and writing with which to consider speculative reconfigurations around The Body. Since 1997 she makes, writes, teaches, mentors and collaborates with humans of various types and technologies and non-humans of numerous divergences including mosses, spiders, the sun, pigs, cell cultures, horses, micro-organisms, copper, salt, piss, blood, bicycles, rivers, landscapes, tundras, rocks, trees, shoes, food, books, air, moon and ravens.

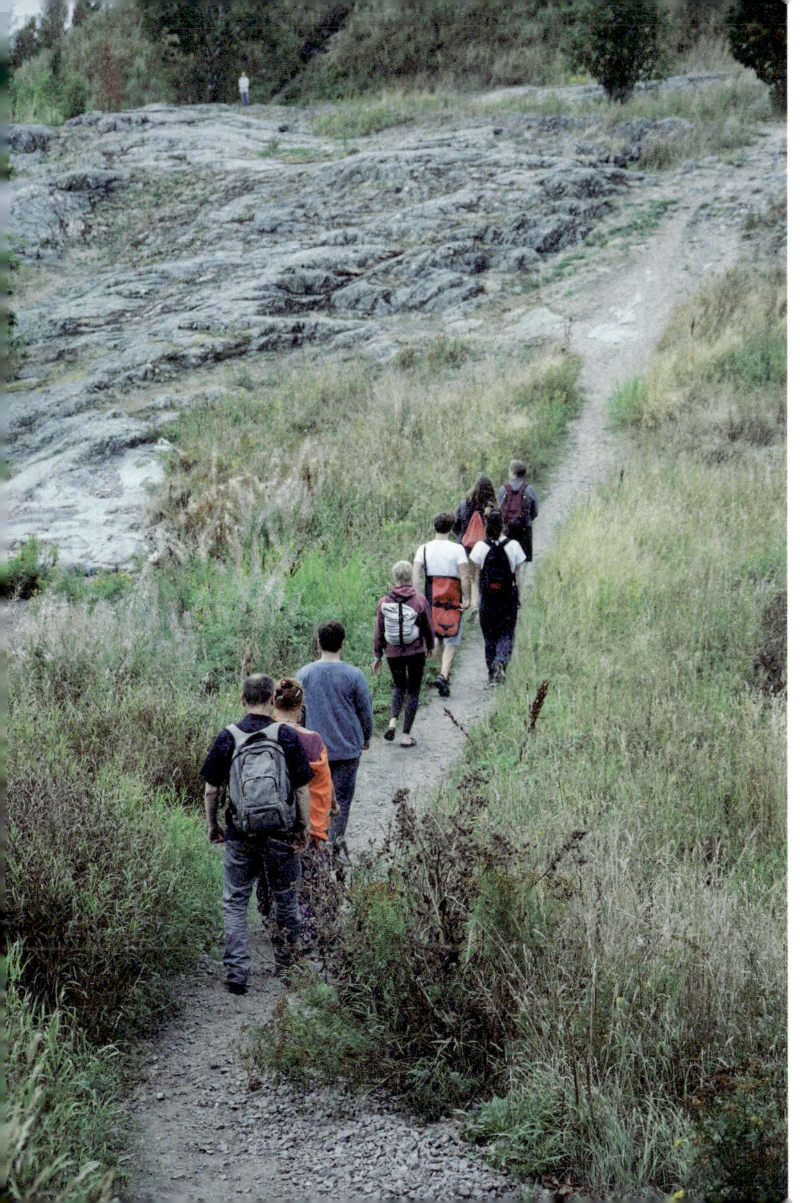

CENTREFOLD

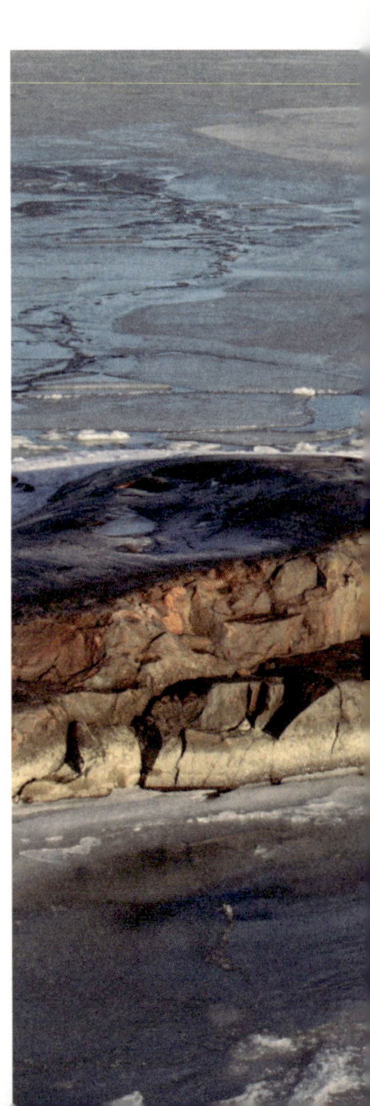

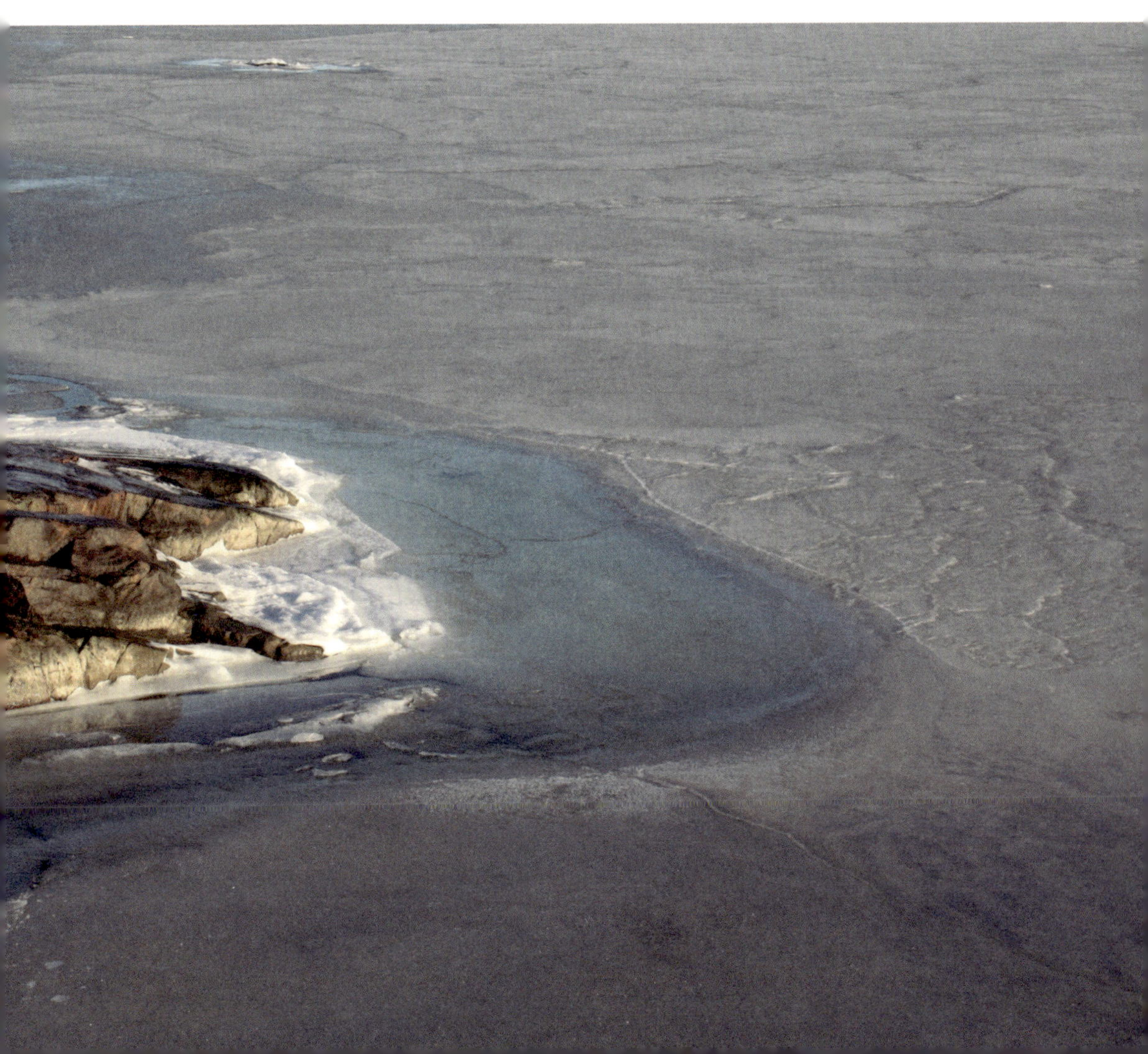

IF YOU SAY

//**Paula Kramer,** February 2018

ONE / SUOMENLINNA

If you say: cold
I say: wind
If you say: snow
I say: white
If you say: blanket
I say: powder

I you say: green
I say: moss
If you say: pink
I say: buoy
If you say: water
I say: a lot

If you say: crust
I say: massive
If you say: rock
I say: with cracks, lines and slants
If you say: surface
I say: reflection
If you say: landscape
I say: territory

If you say: tourists
I say: floods,
but not in this corner
If you say: people
I say: some
If you say: winter
I say: deep
If I say: stillness
A man hollers: are you ok?

If you say: we meet
I say: satisfaction
If you say: rest
I say: yes
If you say: exhaustion
I say: that too
If you say: cold
I say: time

If you say: variety
I say: yes
If you say: multitude
I say: rhythms

If you say: place
I say: expanding

I you say: black
I say: you
If you say: smooth
I say: yes
If you say: where?
I say: Länsi-Mustasaari, northwestern corner.

TWO / *intermezzo* / **PRACTICE**

If you say: what?
I say: movement
If you say: why?
I say: commitment
If you say: to what?
I say: materials, embodiment, emergence of movement

If you say: how?
I say: exposure
If you say: and?
I say: and then we meet
If you say: how?
I say: through movement

And what is relevant?
Patience, spine, matter, form, articulation, repetition

If you say: where?
I say: two places
If you say: which ones?
I say: one island, one city
If you say: same?
I say: different
If you say: interrelationship?
I say: divergent
Yet there is correspondence and sometimes they meet.

If you say: outdoors?
I say: always
If you say: spectacle?
I say: no
If you say: public?
I say: yes

If you say: weather
I say: present
If you say: ground
I say: relevant
If you say: hunger
I say: always
If you say: sensual
I say: yes

If you say: simple
I say: no
If you say: earth
I say: more
If you say: rain
I say: yes
If you say: hale
I say: that also

If you say: extreme
I say: sometimes it helps.

THREE / GROPIUS

If you say: city
I say: home
If you say: entrance
I say: here I am again
If you say: cobblestone
I say: red granite, wet from the rain
If you say: since many years
I say: yes and I see people passing through

Of past, of present.

If you say: trees
I say: comfort
If you say: green
I say: edible
If you say: trunk
I say: coarse
If you say: red
I say: rosehip, plants donated by the US airforce in 1983.

If you say: passage
I say: always
If you say: quiet
I say: lunch break

Where I see oval
You say: circle

Which I finally got now,
from the window above.

If you say: history
I say: I breathe it
If you say: crimes
I say: right here
If you say: tourists
I say: streams

If you say: fence
I say: border
If you say: border
I say: wall
If you say: neighbour
I say: topography
If you say: cameras from all sides
I say: surveillance

Yet, no one has disturbed my working here,
on none of the 29 days I have come.

If you ask: why here?
I say: quite sheltered
If you say: always?
I say: no
If you say: in the middle of everything
I say: yes
If you say: where?
I say: Berlin, Martin-Gropius Bau, south side.

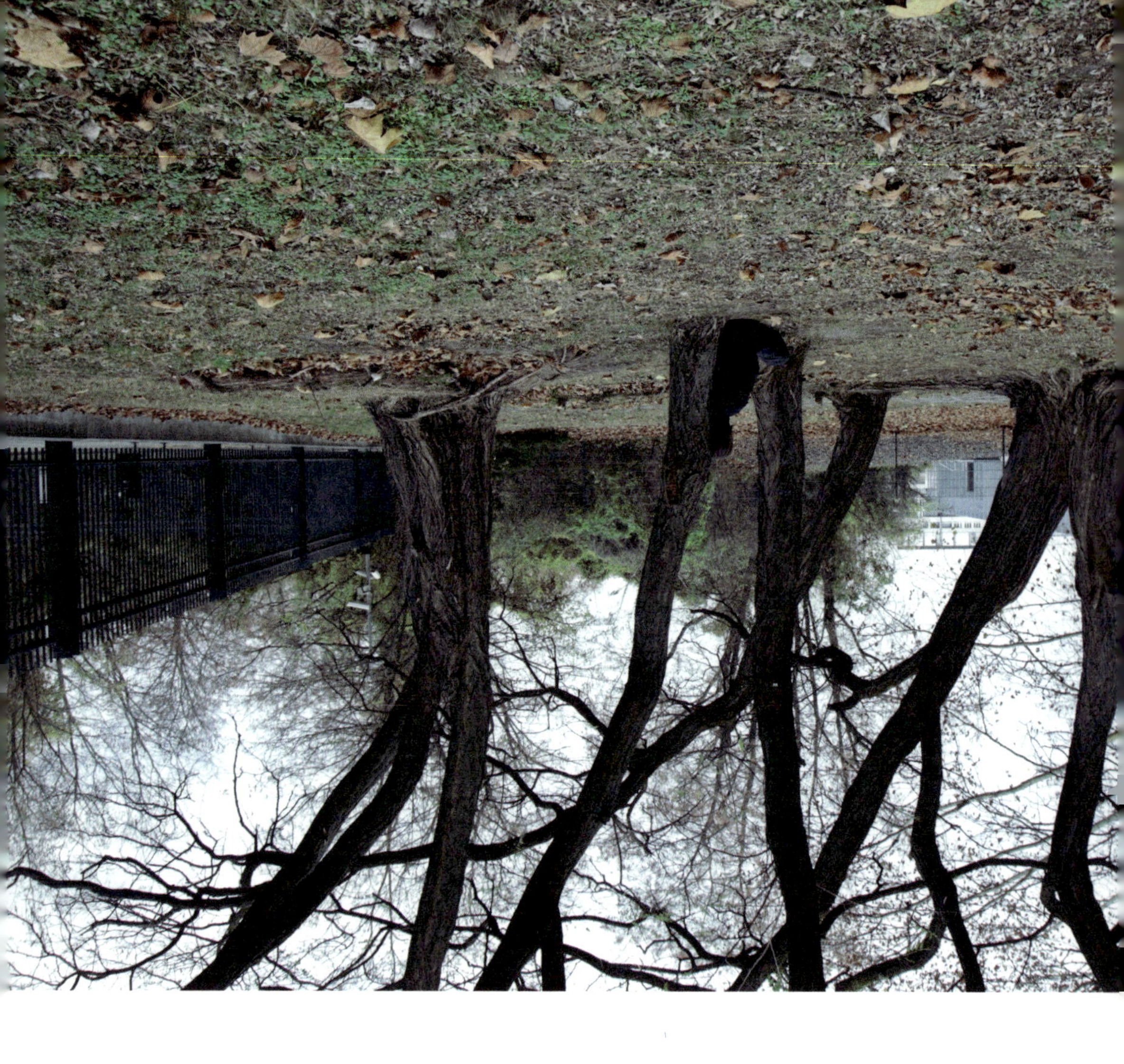

Gropius // Suomenlinna

Paula Kramer

Two Contemplations on Body, Movement
and Intermateriality

tp

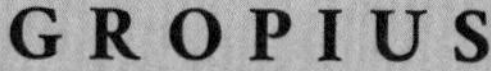
GROPIUS

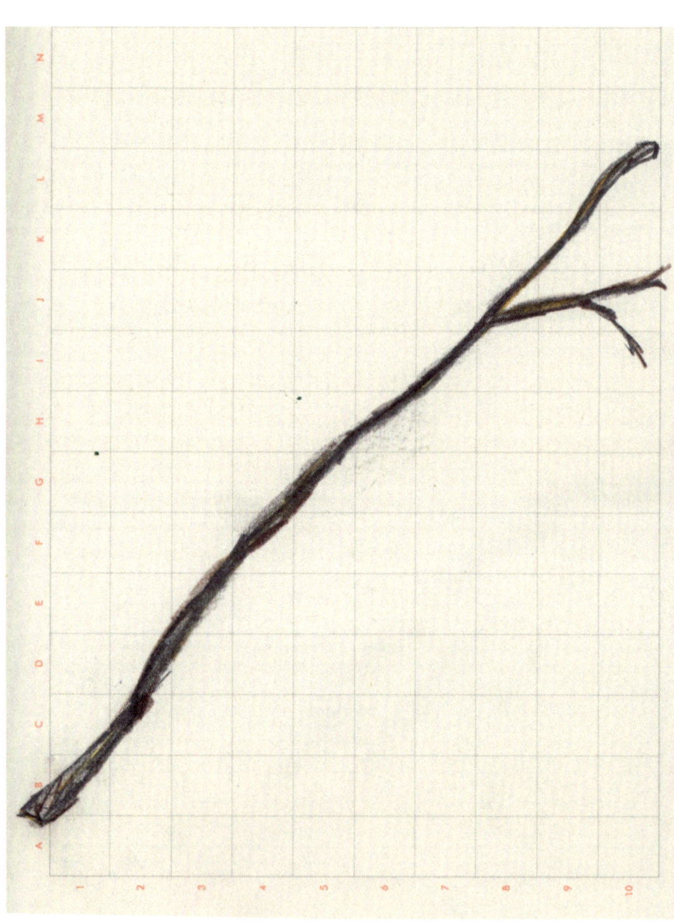

Introduction

This is an invitation to you. To explore narration, poetry and theory born out of specific experiences of moving-dancing, being, eating, choreographing, performing, in and with two sites. One in the middle of a city, one in the middle of a sea.

I invite you to leaf, navigate and flip through this book freely. Finding beginning points, marking your own ends, turning in between. Traversing time and space, travelling to places distant and near, icy and clear, worn and warm. They are all around us, sites with their materials, histories, specificities. Answering the attention we bring to them with numerous gifts.

The structure is easy. This is how we travel:

SITE – PRACTICE – PERFORMANCE

My voice speaks alongside others – experts in history, geology, performance. Additionally, and scattered throughout the book, are *quotes taken from my movement diaries*, strung on a chronological line. Small knots in time, tasting of the then and there. May all of it invite you to see and experience these specific sites (and sites more generally) differently. May it inspire you to hop, skip, jump, walk, crawl, lie, move, dance in unexpected places in unexpected ways. In your way, I mean.

Read both ways.   ¡suɹnʇ əʞɐꓕ

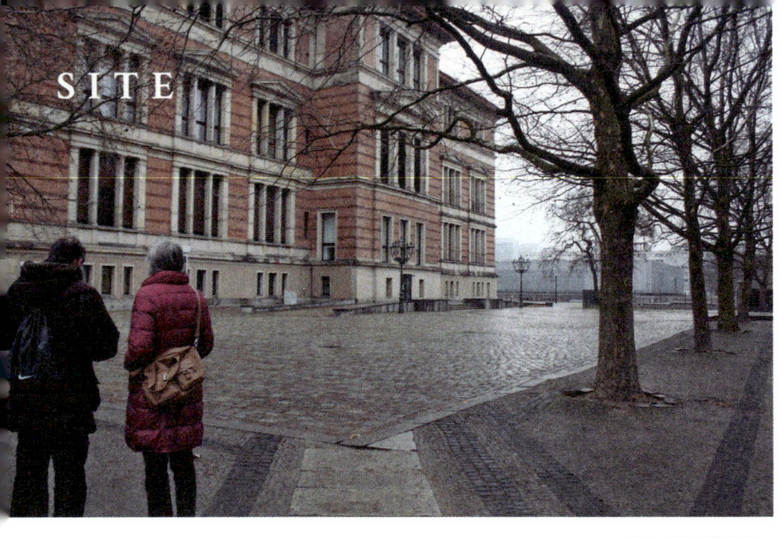

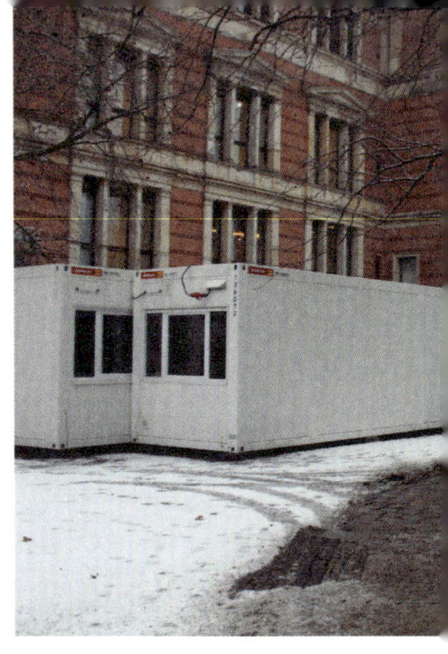

09.12.2016

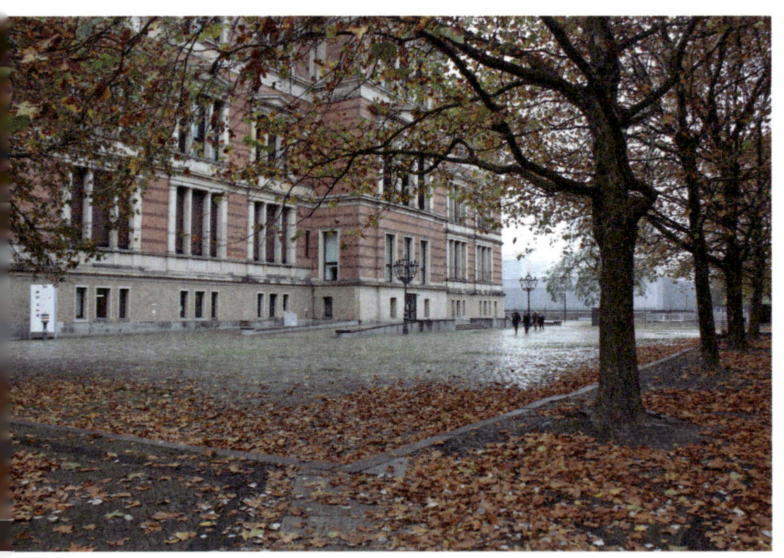

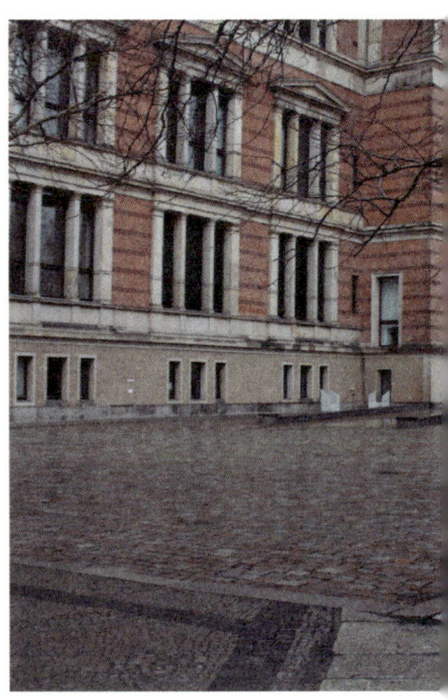

23.10.2017

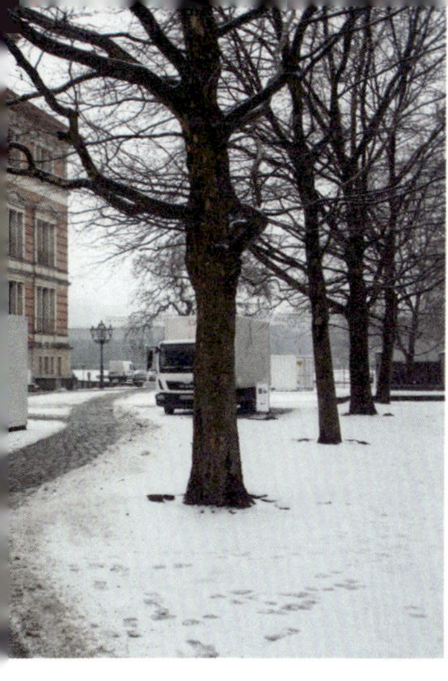

31.01.2017

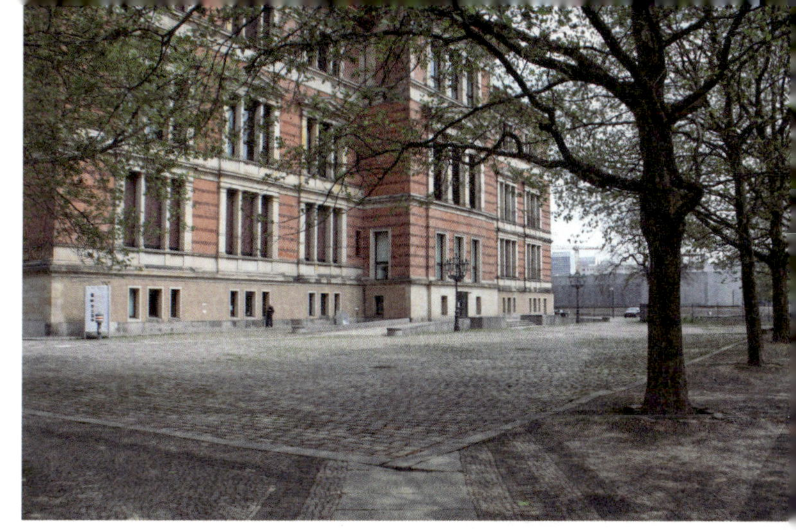

15.05.2017

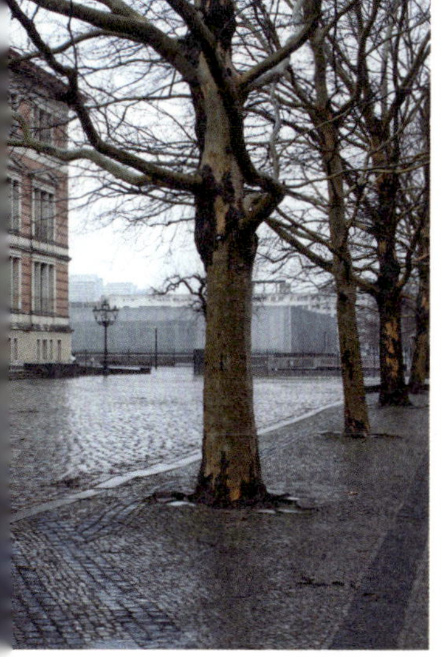

26.03.2019

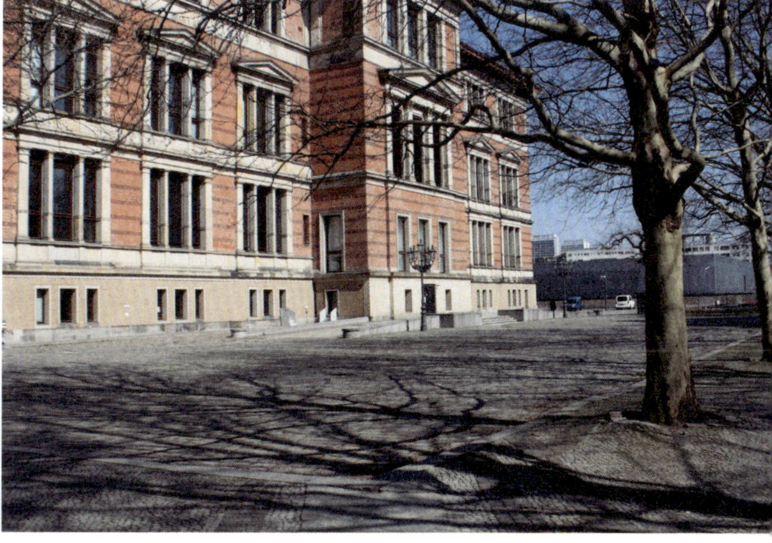

02.04.2019

"In the 1970s, a crumbling and bombed-out shell of what used to be a grand neoclassical structure stood in the middle of abandoned fields filled with rubble and overgrown bushes. Known as the Martin Gropius Bau, this nineteenth-century building was located between Anhalter Straße, Stresemannstraße, Niederkirchnerstraße, and Wilhelmstraße, an area at the margins of West Berlin. A narrow stretch of barren land lay north of this building, between the West and East Berlin Walls. On either side of that patrolled chemical desert stood remnants of once ornate buildings from prewar years, a couple of modern, boxy buildings from the 1920s, and a solid, fortresslike building from the 1930s. The Martin Gropius Bau and these urban fields became the topic of a series of heated debates about national identity that began in the late 1970s and would continue well after reunification."[1]

1. Till, Karen E. (2005): *The New Berlin: Memory, Politics, Place*. Minneapolis: University of Minnesota Press.

GROPIUS
– You Are My Layering

//Paula Kramer

Gropius, you are my layering.

On and around your Südplatz, your plaza on the south side, a lot is going on, each time I come here. Politics and history pile up, and I am only talking about the last one hundred years. Everything coming, and from all sides:

To the north, reconstructed architecture, Renaissance style – since the 1980s (once again) an internationally acclaimed exhibition centre featuring predominantly contemporary art: Martin-Gropius-Bau. The most dominant building of this site, lending itself in shorthand as signifier and title-giving reference for this work: here, we are at Gropius. The Berlin Wall used to press right up against its northern front, a piece of it still standing. Berlin's House of Representatives across the street, once built as the Prussian Parliament with many users in between – including gambling Nazis, the first GDR government and the secret police (Stasi). After the Second World War only ruins and rubble around here.

To the east, one of the top sites of Germany's Nazi regime: behind a high fence lies Topography of Terror, former SS and Gestapo headquarters, now an expansive documentation centre.

To the west, a small rose garden surprises, donated by the US Air Force in 1983 (even today I fail to understand the reasons for this gesture);

behind the roses – Stresemannstrasse. A sizeable road with urban dwellings, amongst them a former hotel, later refugee-accommodation (opened in December 2015, closed at the end of 2019). Sixteen floors, for most of the time with two floors of artists' spaces at the top. Impressive views from up there. Not enough elevators, heightened security downstairs and children hanging out on the ex-hotel floors.

The southern border is delineated by a high fence with security cameras and flags nearby – the Federal Ministry for Economic Cooperation and Development.

Streams of tourists flowing around you. Streets busy with buses, cars and bicycles. A constant meeting of atmospheres, current and historical – tangible here.

And yet, Südplatz itself is surprisingly silent and relatively empty. This site, although deep in the middle of everything, is somewhat undiscovered, hidden. Big trees shelter a small strip of green that is rarely frequented by humans. Purslane, chickweed, rosehip and some elderberry growing all around. Fallen relics of buildings past lying about. A big old metal gate still standing. Catching people's attention every time. A prison gate? An entryway to a former park?

In April 2019, on one of my last days of practice, a fox cuts across the full site, stretching wide, galloping fast. Coming from Stresemannstrasse, ducking under Topography's fence, vanishing into blackthorn. A spider crawls across the pages of my notebook. A crow calls from afar. I note in my movement diary: *the animals are back.*

In the midst of all this I work, move, study. Between November 2016 and April 2019. Finding silence and sorrow, movement and immobility, solace and conflict.

"Why here?" I am asked often. Between trees, behind buildings, next to fences. It's a place I noticed many years ago, as a museum-going person living in Berlin. It intrigued me immediately, with its historical intensity, its romantic greenery, its hidden nature and quietness in the middle of everything. A place to breathe. A colleague's temporary office/mini-studio space on the top floors of the hotel/refugee-accommodation reminded me of this site. At some point I proposed a couple of movement scores, there. For my post-doc I needed a site to work in, to turn to, and this was one place easily at hand. It surfaced first when I scanned my brain for Berlin sites to work in, *now*.

What follows are notes on what sunk into me from this site during the time I engaged with it regularly.

Martin-Gropius-Bau

Gropius. Not Walter, Martin. But we are talking about architecture, still. Large. Impressive. In 1877, the main building of this site is birthed, one hundred years before me. Built by Martin Gropius, great uncle of Bauhaus founder Walter Gropius, together with Heino Schmieden. Largely destroyed in the Second World War. In the centre of Berlin, in the middle of everything. *Every-German-History-and-Current-Affairs-Thing.* Now, that is. In 1979, art critic Heinz Ohff articulates his scepticism about a reconstruction of the building,

2. Taken from a debate aired on German radio (22.08.1979, RIAS), quoted in Kampmann, Winnetou & Weström, Ute (eds.) (1999): *Martin-Gropius-Bau: Die Geschichte seiner Wiederherstellung*, Munich: Prestel, p. 12: "Mit der BVG ist der Bau schlecht zu erreichen, und zu Fuß braucht man mindestens 20 Minuten durch sehr unübersichtliches Gelände."
3. Sound installation 'Unterton' ('Undertone') by Ina Geißler and Fabian Lippert (2012). https://www.museum-der-1000-orte.de/kunstwerke/kunstwerk/unterton

partially because he considers it to be positioned too remotely. He points out that the place is hard to reach on public transport; on foot he estimates a twenty minute walk through "very unwieldy terrain" from other central sites.[2] The wall ran right in front of it, this was the absolute end of West Berlin. Who would come here?

The centre moves. Now, here, once was, now is – a nodal point of Berlin.

This Movement Site, This Hidden Back Yard

Südplatz is an open, round square on the south side of Martin-Gropius-Bau. (Because this square is so purposefully round it is called plaza sometimes in this book, to soften cerebral stumblings. If you can, just think of it as Südplatz.) Reconstruction architect Ute Weström (1999: 18 – see note 2) refers to the south side as the "schmucklose Gartenseite" – the barren side facing the garden. This 'back' served as temporary front and main entrance of Martin-Gropius-Bau for quite some time, during the decades in which the wall blocked the real front to the north. Today, the south side is the back again.

Orientations, facings, move. And the building stands still.

A quiet, wide-open cobblestone circle with a sound installation in its guts, partnered by a cosy, shady, grass and tree assemblage. Ping-ping---ping-ping-ping the manhole covers sound as people cross them.[3] Some are startled, for most it is familiar, some don't notice. I pick rosehips and purslane in the green zones of this site, and sloes in the grounds of Topography.

Der Platz begrüßt mich mit einem grünen Fell. Ich bin lang fort gewesen. Die Schlehenblüte ist lang vorbei, stattdessen alles grün. Sogar die Platanen haben nun Blätter und auch diese zartgrünen Zierbäume vor der Schlehenhecke. Südplatz greets me with a green fur. I've been away for a long time. The blackthorn blossoms are long gone, instead everything is green. Even the plane trees have leaves and also these delicate light green ornamental trees in front of the blackthorn. (10.05.2017)

So different this place, voluminous, totally transformed by growth.

All autumn leaves are gathered in piles, swiff-swiff the sound goes. In weichen Wogen zieht der Wind durch die Blätter der mächtigen Platanenkronen. In soft surges the wind is moving through the leaves of the wide plane tree crowns. (17.05.2018)

Given its placement in the middle of everything, pedestrian traffic on the site is scarce. Visitors cut across to or from Topography, but mostly it is people who work in the vicinity, having lunch on the site. Student groups, some with drawing tasks to do, some sitting and passing the time. Sporadic geocachers, who might think I am a competitor. And sometimes, more so in the summer, people, families, from the refugee accommodation. I am often alone when I am here, or with one, two, three people sitting somewhere on the edges, others crossing the space diagonally, every few minutes, with pauses between.

And yet, the wider area is somewhat hyperactive. Three times I chance upon a demonstration or protest near this site and I am sure there were many others in this period. Many relevant political institutions are located around here, tangible also in these gestures of becoming publicly visible. One gathering I join spontaneously in November 2016, on my second day on site – a flag is flown by Terre des Femmes to commemorate the International Day for the Elimination of Violence Against Women. In May 2018 I join a group that gathers to hand over more than 485,000 signatures to stop the use of glyphosate to Svenja Schulze, Federal Minister of the Environment. Between these two events a protest by the trades union ver.di and workers from a local energy provider takes place, their speeches the audio track of a video I shot on this day.

Democracy, I scribble in my notebook, *also means to be present, to be available, by chance or on purpose, as body in space. (24.11.2016)*

This is a contested site. It has been a contested site, as Ulrich Tempel's text (following this one) details. Severely damaged in the Second World War, Martin-Gropius-Bau was an empty ruin for decades and almost torn down. And even after it was declared a listed monument in 1966, years went by discussing how or even whether it should be reconstructed (a common theme in this city). Several plans for the reconstruction were considered, well known architects like Hans Hollein (Vienna) made proposals that were rejected. Until, in 1977, the proposal of a local architect with the unlikely name Winnetou Kampmann and his partner Ute Weström was chosen and began to be realized. The world itself, I think sometimes, provides the most improbable performances.

I am glad to know of these previous conflicts around site usage, when my own conflict around performing on this site is taking place. I read about the reconstruction struggles in Topography's library just the day before I receive the letter that brings an end to publicly sharing my work on this site. This kept me good company.

An Influential Neighbour: Topography of Terror

Regulatory conflicts around site usage, I know this much, were even more severe on the neighbouring site, Topography. Decades after the Nazi regime had finally been demolished and dismantled and the central buildings for planning and executing their crimes levelled to the ground, architectural battles broke out. Millions of Deutschmarks sunk with Peter Zumthor's original (and grand) plans of 1993[4]. Years of wasteland and denial before that and years of wasteland and immobility afterwards. But eventually the solutions we know today were found.

In 2010, Topography finally opens its doors, a documentation centre for Nazi crimes with a clear, contemplative and functional building planned by Ursula Wilms and landscaped surroundings by Heinz W. Hallmann. A large gravel field resonant of the dire past, bordered behind by blackthorn shrubs that blossom ludicrously in the spring. Behind them, an unkempt Black Locust wood with remnants of a 1970s' *Autodrom* – a kind of parkland-driving-practice-race-track on which one could drive without a licence.

An important signifier on my movement site is a long high fence, today delineating the shared border between Südplatz and Topography. The wind often blows first across Topography, then over Südplatz, bringing

4. Summary of the events here: https://www.topographie.de/en/the-historic-site/the-establishment-of-the-topography-of-terror/

current sounds and presencing the past. All the deaths. All the atrocities. All right here.

A gardener works here, day after day, pulling weeds from between the large gravel stones to maintain a field of stark grey that would become green otherwise. I speak to him early on, we converse about sloes and weeds and Italy.

Topography also houses a wonderful library. It is downstairs, large windows bordering a square courtyard, the heart of the building. Ceiling cut out, light and sky sometimes reflected in the surface of a square on the ground that collects rainwater. A peaceful place that becomes my site-office and writing place; a place for background reading, note taking and being among books. Germany's international guilt and debt transformed: an indispensable documentation centre creates a useful public infrastructure as a side effect.

I am generally startled by the infrastructure near my movement site. Since I tend to work somewhat remotely – near woods, trees, roads, rocks – I am not used to the lockers, cafeterias, toilets, writing desks spread across three major institutions open to the public – Martin-Gropius-Bau, Berlin's House of Representatives and Topography.

The library is never crowded, there is always an expanded sense of time, librarians have time to help, look up information and sometimes bring a book to where I sit. When and how do I find out about context? It comes in waves and phases, light compared to the time I spend on site, moving. But some things I want to know, what was built when, how did this site change face?

Poetic Traces, Past and Present

Persistent inquiries for poetry written on the Topography site bring the archivist Ulrich Tempel into the margins of this project at the end of 2018 – a crossing of paths I am immensely grateful for. At the time I had considered the possibility of threading Topography's presence into my performance through poetry. My trial poem had been 'An mein Kind' ('To my Child') by Mascha Kaléko, read to a witnessing colleague during heavy rain and hail (4.12.2017).[5] Written in Berlin, in the 1930s – yes. But not here. The poet driven into exile in 1938 – yes, but not imprisoned here. Yet to have her voice join with the winds of the past seemed about right for a trial inclusion of poetry. So we sat there, by the south entrance, leaning against the small wall by the stairs, crouched in the rain, half under a black umbrella, water running down my hands. Bettina carrying a camera under her raincoat like a bird that is nesting there. *"Dir will ich meines Liebsten Augen geben ..." (To you I want to pass my loved one's eyes ...).*

I learn from Ulrich Tempel that Dietrich Bonhoeffer's famous poem – today well known as a church hymn – 'Von Guten Mächten' ('By Good Forces') was written in the house prison of Topography and sent in a letter to his then fiancée Maria von Wedemeyer on 19.12.1944. Having graduated from a Dietrich-Bonhoeffer grammar school I am deeply familiar with these lines and at the same time oblivious to where exactly they were written as well as never having heard anything

5. Kaléko, Mascha & Zoch-Westphal, Gisela (2007): *Mein Lied Geht Weiter: Hundert Gedichte.* München: dtv.

about Maria von Wedemeyer who went on to study maths and became a computer scientist in the USA. This poem, however, seems too well known, too overwritten and too often interpreted to be woven into my work, here. And anyway I figure out that it is not a poem that I need, but the associative capacities of an archivist. The search for a poem being only what led me there.

In the end it is an image of ballroom type dancing taking place on Südplatz that he gifts me with, after a few further conversations. I sigh with excitement and relief. For two years elegant women dancing tango, especially one in a purple dress, had already haunted my imagination when moving on this site. I had almost always felt resistant. Elegance? A dress? Tango? None of these appealed to me in terms of the site and all the other ghosts haunting it. Finally this image from my inner eye, the recurring tango tunes and flimsy steps received a frame, a source, an uncanny legitimacy.

This dancy-dancing that for a long time forms part of my on-site practice, I can finally make peace with. There had been a lot of it around here, mostly in indoor buildings as I discover step by step. But also outside, for example on the bordering Europahaus rooftops, of which I found images with 1920s' open-air gymnastic events. And also on this very site, quietly dancing, round and round, couples on a leisurely Berlin afternoon.

Gropius, you *are* my layering.

I still walk into and away from you struck by your density. History and presence, so tangible here. At the same time space to breathe, space to

be, space to dance, space to see. I am grateful for the time you housed
my moving body, regularly visiting, in conversation with your layers,
visible and invisible.

Rahayu.

Slow tango today, the beginning feels
incredibly sublime, der ganze Platz mir zu
Füßen all of Südplatz at my feet. A dance
with the ghosts of the past …

Und dann immer wieder diesem unerklärlichen
Schrecken direkt gegenüber, und sich davon
nicht erschlagen zu lassen. Einmal halte
ich mich an einer Wolke fest, das geht und
ist ganz gut, da bin ich da drüber.

Again and again face to face with these
unexplainable atrocities, and to not
be totally obliterated by them. Once I hold
on to a cloud, this is possible and helps,
this way I am slightly above.
(11.05.2017)

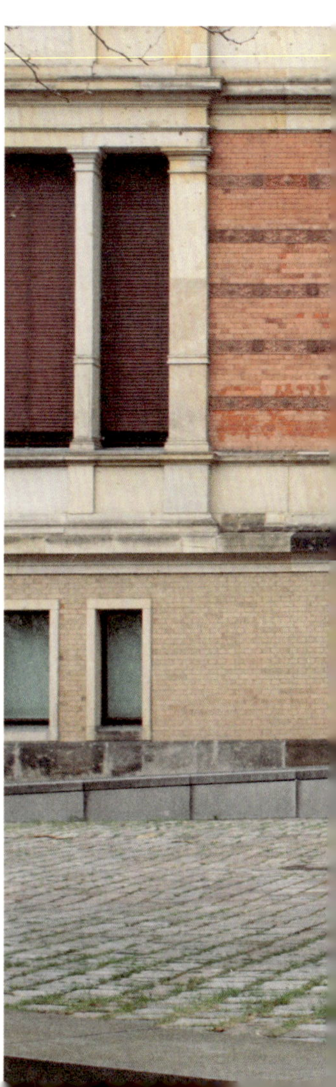

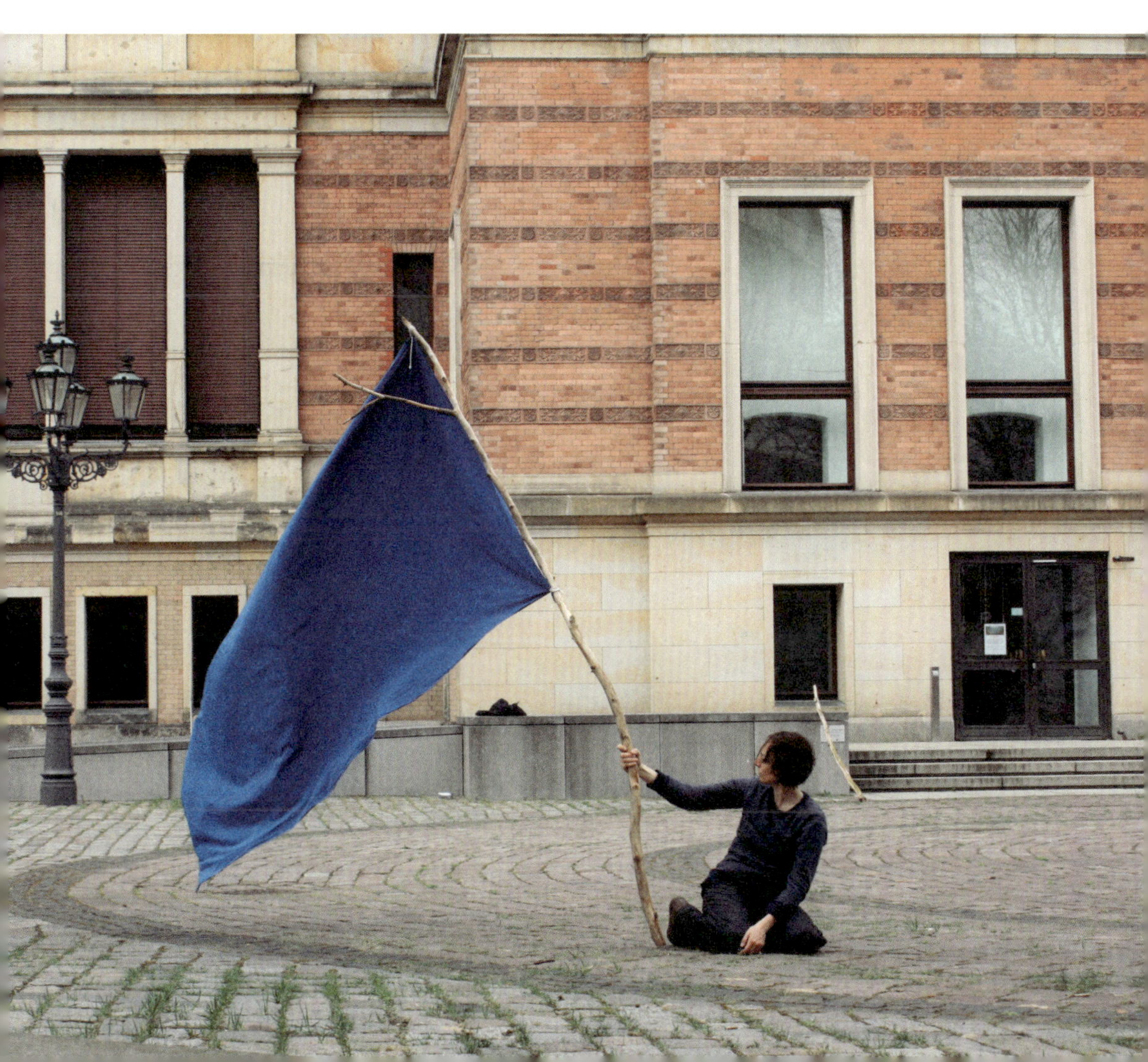

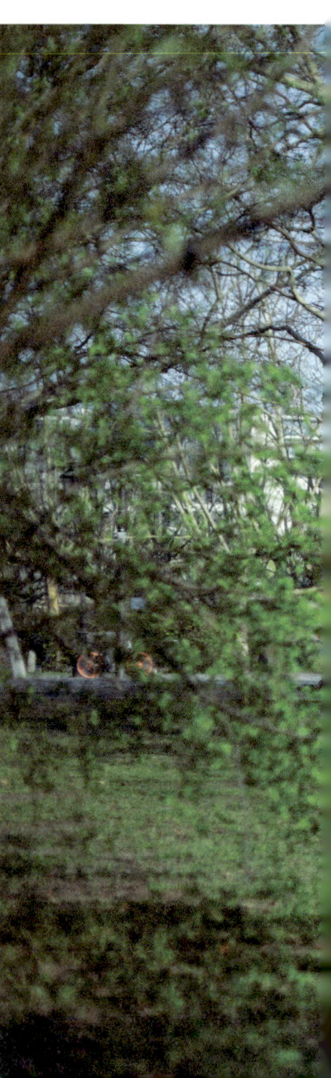

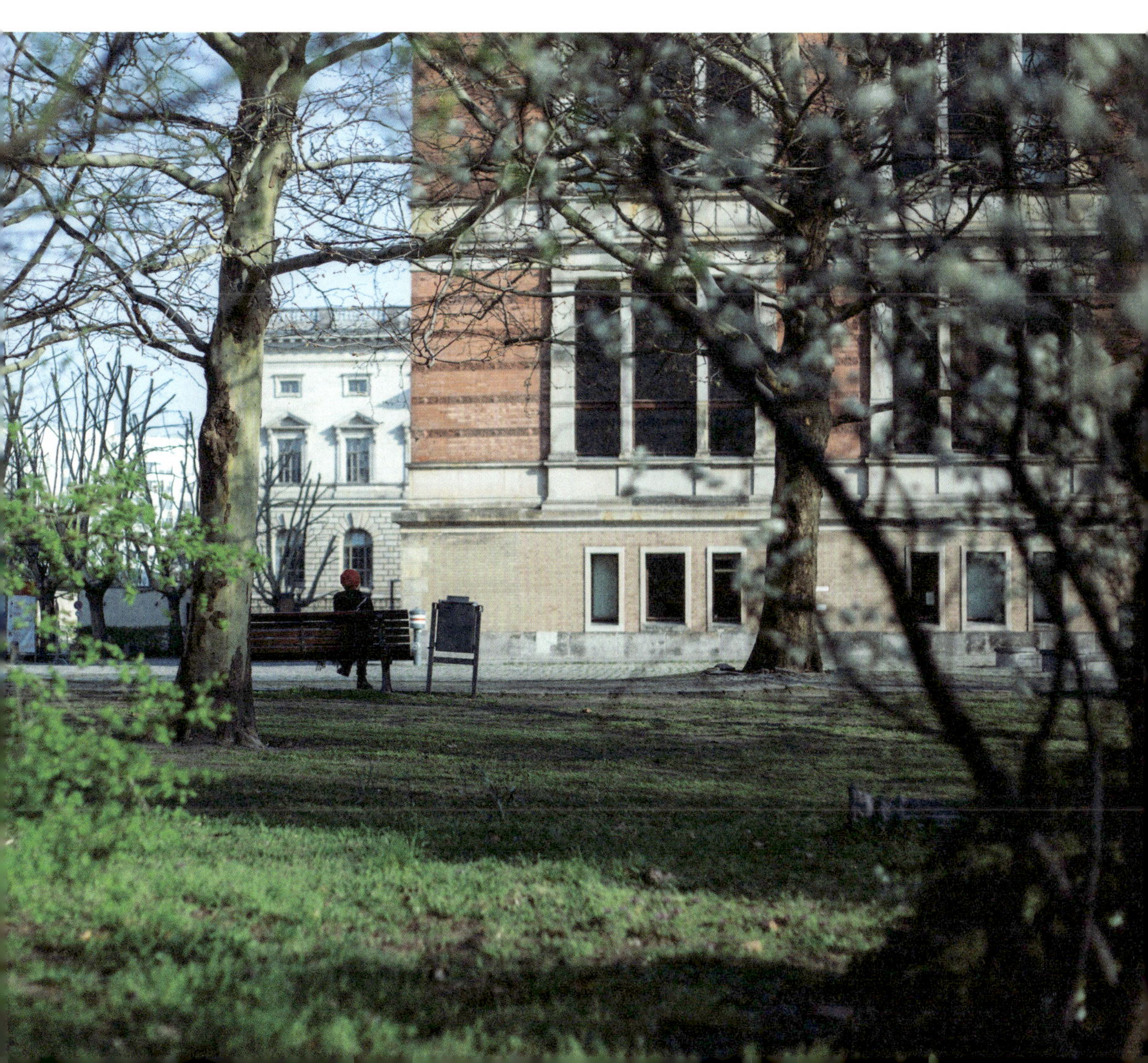

Südplatz: 1910, 1936, 1954, 1984 and today, 2020

// Ulrich Tempel (translated by Michael Thomas Taylor)

A city square in the middle of Berlin. Somewhat hidden. As one approaches it on the walkway coming from Stresemannstrasse, the noise of the city slowly falls away. A clearly structured building facade in Neo-Renaissance style comes into view. The circular design of the plaza and an elegant entryway ramp appear to belong to the building and to date from the time when it was constructed, as do the gas lanterns and a metal gate. But is this really the case? And – why is there a city square at this particular place?

I would like to pursue these questions by opening four 'time windows'. Two detailed maps, an aerial image and three photographs are important documents giving us insight into how a city square developed over the course of ninety years.

Landesarchiv Berlin, Histomap Berlin

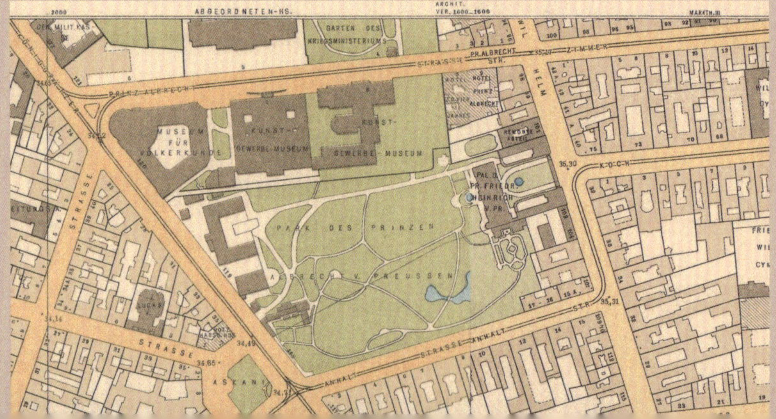

1910

In 1910, what would later come to be called Südplatz (South Side Plaza) is part of the park belonging to the Prinz-Albrecht-Palais.

At the time, roughly two million people live in Berlin, the capital of the German Reich, and the number is still rising. The stately Anhalter Railway Station opens onto a square called Askanischer Platz. Multitudes of people arrive here every day – some with a clear destination and others who are still looking to find their place in the big city. Here and at nearby Potsdamer Platz, we find large hotels, smaller guest houses, and restaurants. The area is characterized by traffic noise, by hustle and bustle. These sounds also penetrate into the Park of Prince Albrecht of Prussia. The adjoining palace, built in the eighteenth century, is named in Straube's General Map of Berlin after one of the prince's descendants: 'Pal[ais] [of] Pr[ince] Friedr[ich] Heinrich [of] Pr[ussia]'.[1] On the western edge of the park, a large U-shaped building can be seen: the stables for the Prince's horses. The area of the park directly in front of the stables is the site where Südplatz will be built more than seventy years later.

In 1910, the palace is still being used by members of the Hohenzollern family and the park is not accessible to the public. However, visitors to the Museum of Decorative Arts (Kunstgewerbemuseum), today's Martin-Gropius-Bau, are probably able to get a glimpse of the park from the museum's exhibition spaces. This building was opened in 1881 and combines a museum, school and library; all three are devoted to promoting the production of arts and crafts. The facades facing east, west, and north are elaborately decorated and designed – subdivided with cornices and embellished with ornaments and images. The south side, however, is not. It is elegantly subdivided, but without the decoration of the other three facades. This difference is still clearly visible today.

1. "Pal[ais] d[es] Pr[inzen] Friedr[ich] Heinrich v[on] Pr[eußen]"; Straubes Übersichtsplan von Berlin in 44 Blättern (Straube's general map of Berlin in 44 sheets) was prepared by the cartographer Julius Straube and published in 1910 (scale 1:4000).

It soon becomes apparent that the impressive building is too small to be a museum, school and library. In 1905, another building is therefore opened to the east of the Museum of Decorative Arts – the School of Decorative Arts (Kunstgewerbeschule), which now also houses the library. The classrooms in the south wing offer a wonderful view of a green landscape – in the midst of the metropolis. Photographs show the park to be heavily wooded, and the students in the workshops on the mansard roof can look down into treetops and beyond.

1936

What will later become Südplatz is the courtyard of the buildings that have gone up on Stresemannstrasse. A large part is occupied by the Theater im Europahaus.

Compared to 1910, the situation twenty-six years later has changed. The Europahaus complex of offices, cafés and entertainment venues has been built on the western side of the site. In the mid-1920s, the Hohenzollern family sold the western section of their park for development. Today, in 2020, one reminder of this property boundary is a metal gate that remains an important visual reference in the Südplatz area. In 1936, the building of the Museum of Decorative Arts is used by other museums. At the end of the Europahaus complex on Stresemannstrasse, a sign with the words "Europa Tanz Pavillon" calls out to passers-by. The dance pavilion seats 600 people, has a gallery, is decorated in silver and orange, and is directly connected to the Café Europahaus.

A photo from a Berlin image archive shows a summer dance garden, situated directly behind the dance pavilion and the café. People are spread out through the space, sitting at tables; there are sunshades, evening lighting, and a round dance area with five couples dancing. This summer garden can only have existed for a few years, because – as can be seen on the 1936 map – in the

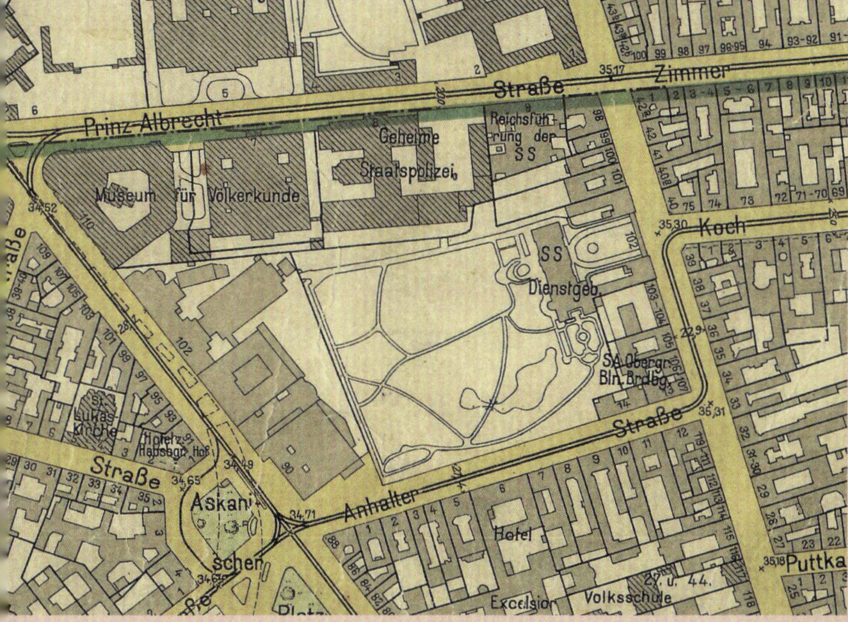

Landesarchiv Berlin, Histomap Berlin

mid-1930s this area was covered by a large cuboid building that extends nearly to the boundary with the Museum of Decorative Arts. This building, a steel and glass construction, provides space for the Theater im Europahaus, also known as the Palmengarten (Palm Garden).

In May 1933, soon after the Nazis come to power, the newly formed Secret State Police or Gestapo (Geheime Staatspolizei) moves into the former School of Decorative Arts. During World War II, the building is destroyed and the ruins are later removed – opening up an area that today belongs to the Topography of Terror Documentation Centre (Topographie des Terrors). From May 1933 to June 1934, the Gestapo shares the building with the art library but finally succeeds in claiming the entire complex. By August 1933, nineteen individual cells have been installed in the basement floor of the south wing on the park side. With the installation of the prison cells, the boundary wall between the park and the site of the School of Decorative Arts takes on a new meaning; it is fitted with a screen and adjoins the yard of this 'house prison', as the Gestapo called it. This courtyard is located only a few metres away from the metal gate that still exists today. Beginning in 1934, various central SS offices move into the adjacent buildings, including the former Prinz-Albrecht-Palais.

Most of the prisoners are political persecutees who are handed over after the Gestapo's investigations to the judiciary or sent to concentration camps; in other words, most of them are imprisoned here only temporarily. Looking at the map, it is striking that only around 100 metres separate the cells of the house prison and the Europa-Tanzcafé. The Theater im Europahaus, newly built in the mid-1930s, is even closer. There is thus very little distance between the place where so many opponents of the National Socialists suffered and the spaces of distraction and amusement for Berlin's residents and visitors.

1954

What later became Südplatz is once again a building courtyard. The floor plan of the Theater im Europahaus is still evident.

In the 1954 photo, the partially destroyed buildings on Stresemannstrasse can be seen quite clearly: the Deutschlandhaus on Askanischer Platz, next to the eleven-storey Europahaus, and finally the lower buildings, which only have a narrow entry passage next to the Museum of Völkerkunde. The striking round building at the corner of Niederkirchnerstrasse still functions as a point of reference in the wider urban environment.

The border that was created in the mid-1920s when the Hohenzollerns sold part of their land and divided the park is still clearly visible. Beyond the wall, which appears to be intact as a boundary, a wasteland extends to Wilhelmstrasse, where various remnants of buildings exist alongside spontaneously created paths: the remaining ruins of the Prinz-Albrecht-Palais at the intersection of Kochstrasse are clearly visible, and on Niederkirchnerstrasse a garage complex built for the Gestapo in the 1930s is easy to make out. The building of the School of Decorative Arts, which housed the Gestapo headquarters from 1933, is in the process of being demolished. The Museum of Decorative Arts is a ruin.

What later became Südplatz is still separated from Stresemannstrasse by the lower building of the Europahaus complex. The perimeter of the Theater im Europahaus is still visible on the ground, but the destroyed steel and glass construction has been removed. At the time, nothing suggests that this site south of the Museum of Decorative Arts would be given a completely new function thirty years later.

Geoportal Berlin

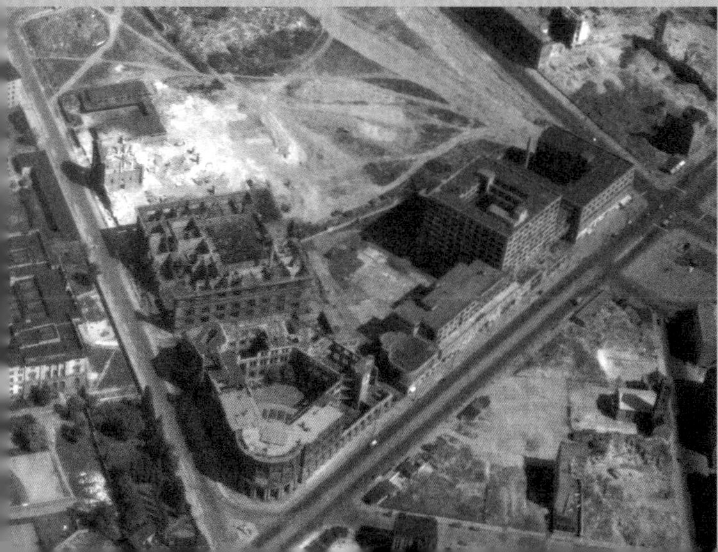

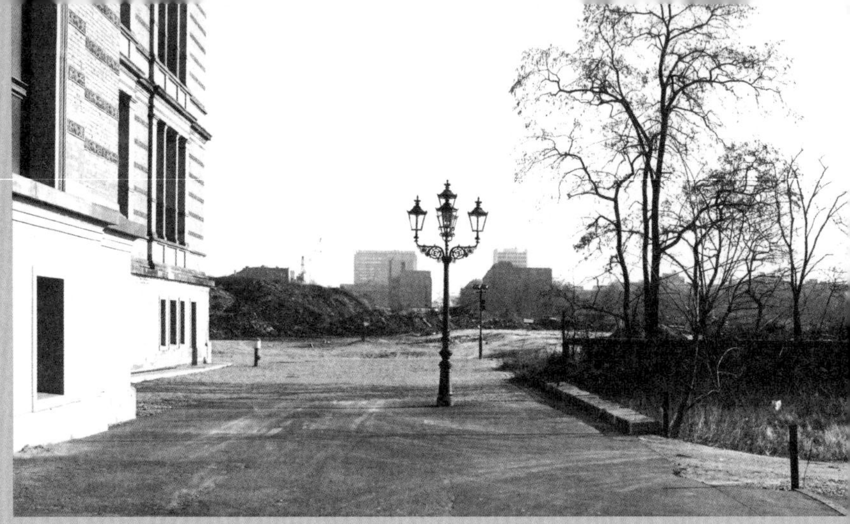

Margret Nissen / Stiftung Topographie des Terrors

1984

Südplatz is on the brink of its construction.

Two photographs by Margret Nissen document the condition of the site in 1984. The area directly in front of the south facade has been paved. Mock-antique street lamps in the style of gas lamps have been added. The wall that divided the park when the Hohenzollerns sold some of their land still exists but has now lost any function. In 1984, the largest part of Südplatz is covered with steppe-like vegetation.

The construction of the Berlin Wall in 1961 transformed the entire area around Anhalter Railway Station into a peripheral location in relationship to what then became West Berlin. It was therefore a landmark decision in the 1970s to reconstruct the building of the Museum of Decorative Arts. In August 1981, the exhibition 'Prussia: An Attempt to Take Stock' ('Preußen – Versuch einer Bilanz') is opened in the building, now renamed Martin-Gropius-Bau.

Part of this stocktaking is also the direct view of the adjoining area, where the Gestapo and SS headquarters were located. A room in the eastern wing of the building allows visitors to look over the wasteland that has emerged since the war ended.

During the planning for the reconstruction, a decision is taken to make a serious intervention in the structure of the building. The entrance is moved to the south side (which had previously been without an entrance) since the street on the north side is now part of the East Berlin district Mitte and the Wall almost reaches the sidewalk. This is the moment when Südplatz is born. Demands for a more prominent entrance are rejected and only a simple door is inserted.

The buildings on Stresemannstrasse that originally housed the dance pavilion and the large café were demolished at the end of the 1960s. Coming from Askanischer Platz and Anhalter Railway Station, a pedestrian can now see the building of the Museum of Decorative Arts and its south and west facades, and, beginning in 1981, direct access to the structure, now the Martin-Gropius-Bau, is also possible. During the preparations for the 750th anniversary celebration of Berlin in 1987, designs for Südplatz are drawn up, giving the plaza its characteristic round shape. The architects in charge of Martin-Gropius-Bau describe Südplatz in the large illustrated volume they produced to take stock of their work: "The design of the forecourt with the outside facilities and a generous ramp visually guides visitors to the entrance, so that even high-ranking guests of honour driving up in limousines were spared the feeling of having to enter the building through a rear entrance."[2] The intention is therefore (also) to create a prestigious entrance setting – including the possibility of arriving by car and turning round.

After the fall of the Wall, Niederkirchnerstrasse is quickly reopened to traffic, rendering obsolete (almost overnight) the entrance constructed during the 1980s. Renovation work in the 1990s finally restores the original state of the

2. Kampmann, Winnetou & Weström, Ute: 'Rekonstruktionen im Außenbereich', in: Kampmann, Winnetou & Weström, Ute (eds.) (1999): *Martin-Gropius-Bau: Die Geschichte seiner Wiederherstellung*, Munich: Prestel, pp. 42-87, here p. 48.

building from its first construction, re-enabling access from the north side. However, the elaborate design of Südplatz on the south side has been preserved to this day.

And today – 2020: In the morning, I often choose the route via Südplatz to reach the Topography of Terror Documentation Centre, which was built on the grounds of the Gestapo and SS headquarters. There are usually very few other people walking about. During the summertime, employees of the Martin-Gropius-Bau might take advantage of the quiet offered by the square for an impromptu lunch. Sometimes school classes pass through, or individual tourists traverse the space. The metal gate still exists – a reference to the division of the property in the 1920s – that presumably served as a side entrance to the SS and Gestapo complex and today forms the boundary of the Topography of Terror Documentation Centre.

This is a designed place that asks to be read. With surroundings full of history, Martin-Gropius-Bau is an architectural testament from the time when large museum collections originated. The Europahaus stands as a symbol of the Berlin of the Weimar Republic. And right next to it is the site where the Nazis organized persecution and mass murder, where many people were imprisoned at Gestapo headquarters and exposed to Gestapo terror.

Ulrich Tempel // is the archivist of the Topography of Terror Foundation. He studied history and German at the Technical University of Berlin, where he passed the first state examination; he later qualified as a Diplom-Archivar (FH) while working at the Topography of Terror. For several years, he has been working on the visual tradition of the Topography of Terror site, among other topics.

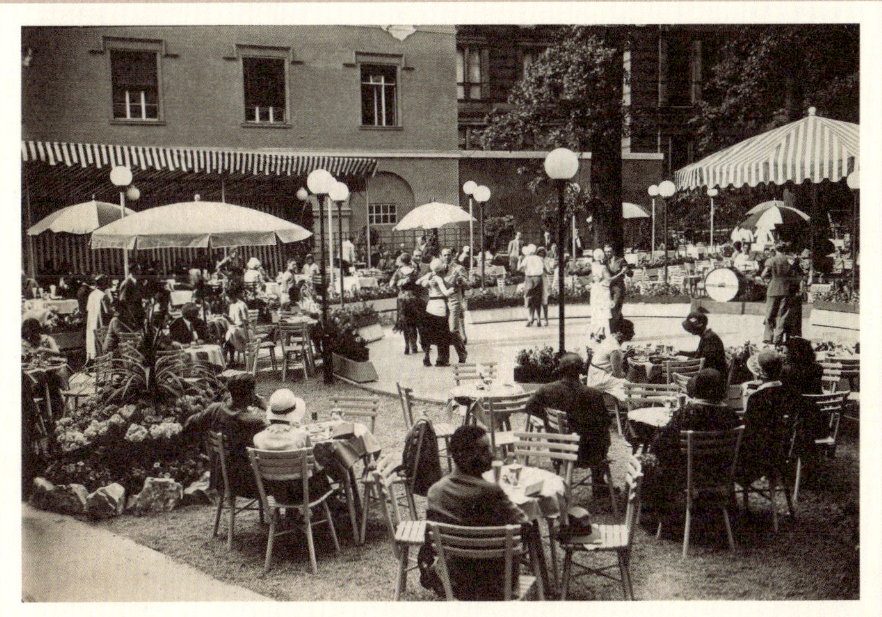

Dance Café Europahaus, Berlin 1932

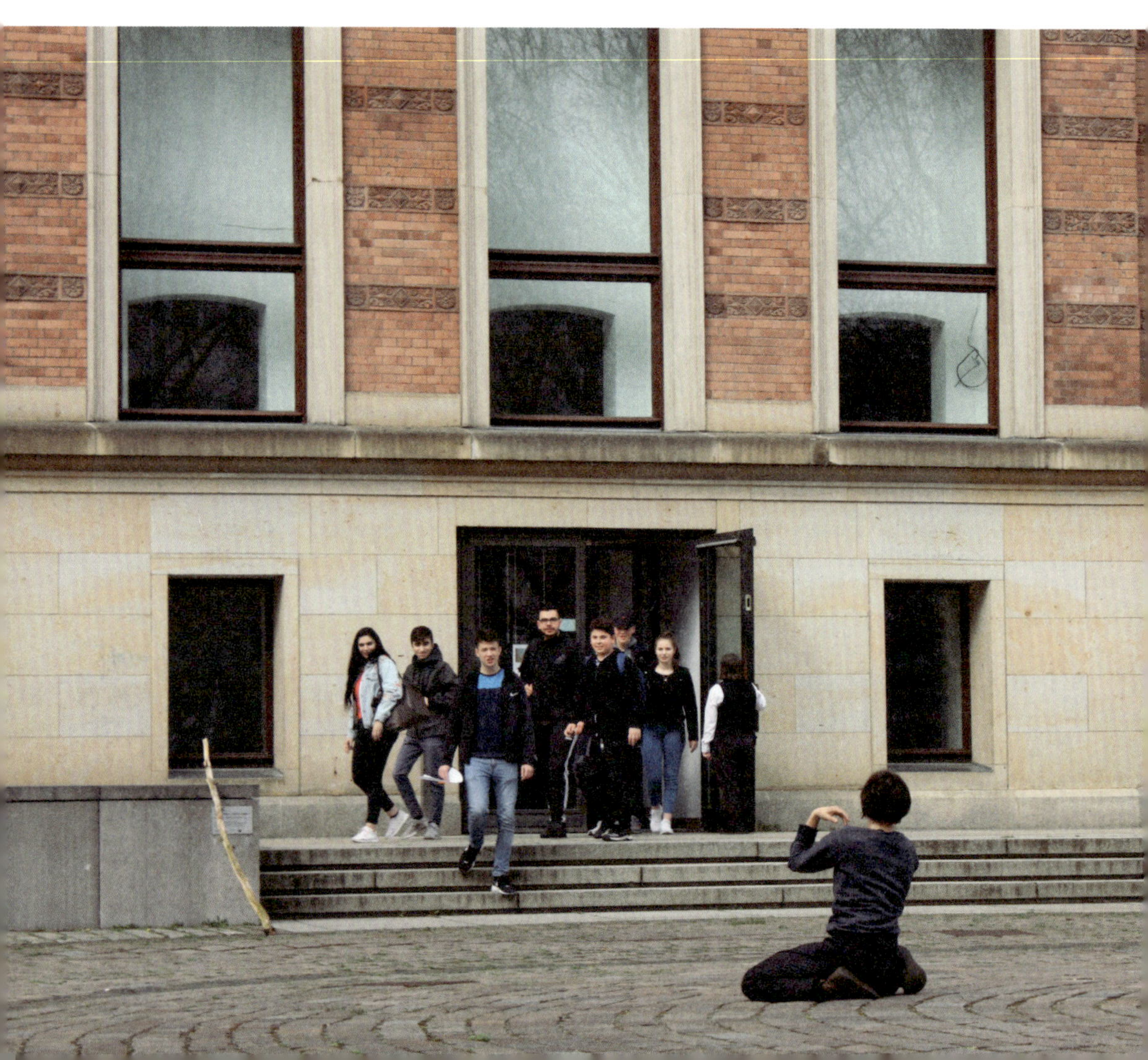

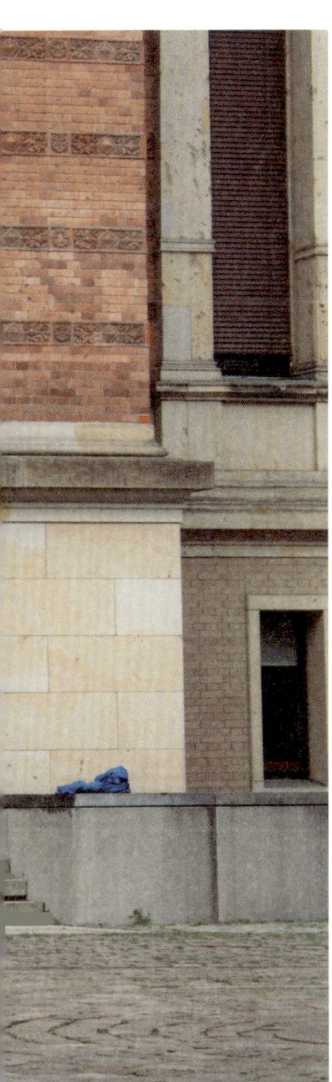

PRACTICE

Es ist doch wirklich fast nichts schöner
als sich im städtischen Raum 'komisch' zu
bewegen und dabei doch ganz friedlich
zu sein, ohne Agenda, ohne Kampf. Einfach
nur so da, am Rand der Norm entlangtanzend.
Hardly anything is better than moving
strangely in urban space, whilst being quite
peaceful, without agenda, without fight.
Just being there, dancing on the edge of
the norm.

Hier ist ein wunderbarer Arbeitsplatz.
This is a great place to work.
(17.11.2016)

GROPIUS
– Practising Movement

//Paula Kramer

I begin to move here in 2016 and work as a soloist. First more regularly (weekly), then less so (monthly, sometimes more often, sometimes with longer breaks). Then rehearsing (every day) and then performing. Or so I thought. I spend around 57 days on site, the first day is November 17th, 2016, the last April 6th, 2019.

At ease it sounds like this:

> *Every person crossing here leaves a rhythm, a trace, and with that I am having fun moving. (20.12.2016)*

With a sense of struggle, more like this:

> *I notice that I dread the beginning, to begin moving, here in public. It is always an effort, no doubt. (24.11.2017)*

Seasons play a crucial role and many of my notes begin with the weather – the grey, endless windy grey of autumn and winter in Berlin, the constant soft rain, the heavy rain, some hail. The warmth of spring, the strong spring sun, the high sky of summer, again and again the wind on site. I note the size and colour of leaves, the peeling bark of the plane trees. Animals populate the site, the small world of insects, the birds above, a fox cutting across, only once.

In the beginning I take extended walks, orbiting around Martin-Gropius-Bau and including, in figure eights and wider circles: the Topography grounds, the House of Representatives across the street, the immediate neighbourhood. In parallel I come close, make physical contact with what is here – trees, pavement, walls, stairs, fence, grass, roots, earth. I become acquainted with where I am. Opening my senses, noticing what comes in. Following. With time the walks become less, the circles smaller. I have enough of an extended sense of this site stored in my body through roaming its surroundings and begin to focus more on the direct, specific site: Südplatz.

I note and notice many a thing. When I lie on my back and raise my arms towards the sky, my shoulder blades can distinguish the varying surfaces of the cobblestones that pave the square. When directing my attention towards the gaps between the rocks, the green and brown seams invite moveabilty and articulation into my body. The big green leaves are reflected in Gropius's windows in a particular way.

From the miniscule to the grand, many perspectives open here. With body and site touching, intermingling, intermaterialising. Making movement together. With animals, and wind, and traffic noise, and buildings, and trees. With concrete forms and the whole wide sky, with atrocities past and current politics, with daily life, small critters, planet earth and grand architecture coexisting side by side.

I begin standing, next to a tree. Standing, just standing, until wind and coarse-woven bark and the wind-bent branches speak to my muscles and my body twists and shifts. Especially the left shoulder. I am with wind bent and tree forms. Then moving down and bending, towards the ground, earth – I don't quite remember fully. Some earth, yes, some planet earth and small insects, critters, too. Close to the ground, grasses and weeds. (07.06.2018)

When I find something edible on site, I eat it. Purslane, nettles, chickweed. Small leaves and some shrubs populate, configure, make this site. And big trees, mighty crowns, standing bare like menorahs in the winter, producing big leaves in May that fall late in the year – plane trees. I preserve small amounts of wild harvests to be shared during performance-events and otherwise.

Sloes become > sloe vodka, sloe juice, sloe jam.
Rosehips become > Rosehip tea, rosehip jam – and so on.

Eating the site is a collateral happening, something I engage with throughout, without too much meaning-making and classification. An ingestion, an intermaterial meeting, yes. Site and body mingle. Time becomes tangible. The first harvest of sloes on Topography was grand, the second non-existent. I am glad my livelihood does not depend on these erratic patterns. Rosehips filled the sloe-gap in year two. "It's nice to eat the landscape", Sophia will say in year three.

Most often I begin under the trees, the place where I feel most sheltered, least vulnerable. Already on my third day on site I note: *the norm-deviation-behaviour-line seems to be softer among the trees. (30.11.2016)* It stays this way until the end: *it is again the trees that offer solace, structure, protection, companionship, reason to move. (02.04.2019)* I can do whatever I want here. Can I? Never quite possible, but close enough. A relative sense of relaxation, under the trees. This feeling returns and remains. Under the trees is my safe space.

"Still a surprising amount of leaves on the trees. And now it has already stopped raining. Paula actually blends so well into this image, in this kind of half-light-half-dark, she could be here all day long, it would not bother anyone and attract no one's attention." (Susanne Martin, translated audio recording, 03.12.2018)

In the round cobblestone circle, the plaza, I am always hyper visible, exposed. In the arena. The space is wide open, surveillance cameras on all sides. In between, small figure me, moving. I am constantly documented and wonder who watches me. What do I dare to do here, today? How much or not do I have a sense of freedom? Can I move without self-restriction in response to what I see, sense, hear, feel, think, imagine?

I lie, I crawl, I run in circles. I rest my head on stonewalls, I crouch next to stairs. I balance on small walls, I kneel. I move, I dance, I carry a stick. I wear mostly raingear (all black). In the warm and dry months, simple movement clothing.

Early on, in December 2016, elegant ladies appear in my imagination, crossing the square. I dance a fleeting tango with the wind (without knowing anything much about tango). I am irritated and for a long time struggle with a constant reappearance of a woman in a purple dress dancing tango. At the same time I enjoy her flimsiness, the appearance of character, a taste of the 1920s. Who would not like to stand at the edge of a bar, leaning slightly, feeling all elegant and metropolitan? But it is not quite 'me' (in raingear, the crawling woman). And also, it is Topography I see and feel quite present when I work on Südplatz, especially near the fence, and a mix of sorrow, shame, pain and cruelty in my body that I cannot quite reconcile with tango and elegant ladies. But again and again I step, step, step across the site and have a taste of people crossing this site before Nazi rule in my body.

In 'Testlauf' ('Trial Run'), a small 1:1 performance experiment, I step these steps but in the end this particular movement reference vanishes from the final ~~performance~~. But it hangs around, shaping first this site and then my site work and I am glad my physical radar caught its signal.

Daily life is another point of relationship on this site, everyday social practices, ingrained, happening, here. Manifest for example when working, separated by a fence, alongside the gardener taking care of the Topography grounds. I often see him kneel, over there, eliminating weeds from the enormous gravel field. If anyone physically knows this site, the gardener does, I think to myself. He becomes a familiar body, doing bodily practice, a moving point of reference. There are also gardeners/city cleaners in orange gear on the Gropius side of the fence, often around when I am, raking autumn leaves, cutting rose bushes, brushcutting the green fur of the square and so on, and so on, and so on.

There is a moment in January 2017 when it feels like the world is simply unfolding, in its very own way, hyper tangible here, in this moment. On one side of the fence the gardener is weeding, on the other I am dancing, and next to me builders are carrying stuff, unloading a truck with Berlinale materials. Three worlds next to each other, happening simultaneously, unrelated-related.

Yet I am also periodically troubled by questioning the use of making art, faced with such fully sanctioned and recognisable outdoor practices as urban landscaping/cityscaping or building/loading/unloading. *I keep asking myself what I do with this art. Of course. I see the gardener, he gardens, and I? (09.12.2016)*

At the same time, I have total certainty that I as a dancer need to dance right here, in between these other practices, as a means of creating space. Space for thinking, acting, feeling, being. Dancing as a guardian of freedom, protecting and creating room to move and manoeuvre. Dancing as a way of practising alternatives.

It is not always easy, but this line of pondering its use and simultaneously vigorously stepping into art stays alive across my whole working time and develops all the way into my final score. Here I feel the company of the big branch on my back as a structure, as a thing, as a burden and as a task that I (we) bring to this world. And in shimmering meaning-making, doing, moving I physically explore: the task of art to keep spaces open. To keep spaces open.

I am also – time and again – taken by how the site moves all by itself, how correspondences, synchronicities, liveliness happens, always. I sometimes don't need to do much beyond taking note and sometimes am spun into the stories the site tells.

When people cross this site, they always take the diagonal. The sound installation pings. Groups of schoolchildren sometimes (rarely) but then suddenly appear out of nowhere. I once work with a group of colleagues on site, with an invitation to practise alongside. Suddenly everything is full of children with drawing tasks. They arrive exactly when we begin and leave exactly when we stop (06.03.2017). The rhythms and sounds of the site, the beeping and noises of the city traffic – all accompany and seep into my movement.

The moment I stop, people start walking. (23.10.2017) // Gerade als ich auf den Platz trete wird der letzte Berlinale Container abgefahren, irgendwie ist es besser so, die Bahn wieder frei. Just as I step on site the last Berlinale container is removed, maybe it is better this way, more space to move again. (02.03.2018) // Ein Mann mit grüngefärbtem Bart schiebt sein Fahrrad vorbei und zwölf lange Latten werden reintransportiert. A man with a green beard is pushing his bike across the square and twelve long boards are carried inside. (17.05.2018)

On one of my last days on site builders working on the ministry grounds see me standing under the trees and finally call out to me: "Are you looking for the small paper roll? It's in the other one!" I try to tell them that I'm not on a geocaching mission, but my voice hardly reaches them, they insist on pointing out where the roll is and since I've never been able to find this geocache (even though I knew it was there, somewhere) I thought: now is the moment!

And really, in one of the trees – "Higher!" they shout – I find a tiny paper roll held in a plastic container, camouflaged with masking tape. It's a long list with many small boxes in which people can put their names. I am surprised by how many names there are, almost every day there is someone who has left a name and a date. So now I know. This small item is much more visited and better taken care of than I would ever have guessed.

And the shadows of course, moving across the site, and the leaves growing and falling, each year again.

This site is layered, as all sites are, and through my attending more layers appear. The layers of history, the layers of materials, the layers of space. History floods me immediately, maybe slightly less over time, but periodically still and always again, in waves. The horizontal organization of the site becomes familiar soon after, from the ministry fence to Gropius's back entrance, from the footpath from Stresemannstrasse to the Topography fence. Green space and separating bench-wall; open square and entrance arrangement. Footpath diagonal, plaza circle, fence line. Over time and with many visits a vertical organization also unfolds, for me, personally, as follows:

> the high sky
> the plane trees
> the human standing
> being in between
> and crawling
> on the cobblestone up to the low semi-circular stone bench (~ 45 cm)
> then lying
> and directly under the cobblestone (or grass)
> and deep, deep down – under earth

At some point I notice: I work more easily here from the notion of saying good-bye.

Imagine: this is the last time I move here. This is the last time to ever place myself in the infinite streams of now and then, here. This is the last time I am seen here; this is the last time I make this effort; this is the last time I try to grasp the ungraspable, meet the unmeetable, here. This opens my senses, helps me relax, makes it all more fun, lighter. It is the last time.

It affectively charges my body, it gives me strength, it makes me less vulnerable.

> *This wondrous place in Berlin, I will never move here again. This wondrous place in Berlin, I will never move here again. It is somehow easier, to look at the whole thing from the perspective of saying farewell. The performance as a moment of parting. (02.03.2018)*

This is one of my magic spells for dealing with 'being seen'. A way of handling the surveillance cameras, the exposure. If someone were to tell me to stop, it would not matter. It is my last time, anyway.

Only once in this city, and that was on another site, have I experienced passers-by calling the police in the context of movement practice. Three women, between lying and standing slightly bent, moving in a green public space – it might have looked somewhat odd. But never on this site. No one, apart from kids, a couple of interested tourists or one of the men working on or around the site as caretakers, gardeners, builders, ever came to speak to me: *Allet OK bei Ihnen? Keen gesundheitliches Problem? Weil sie da so liegen! Everything OK with you? Are you ill? Because you are lying here like this! In a friendly voice. Of having and giving shelter.* (17.05.2018)

No one stops me waving a blue flag on the oval, crawling in raingear, sleeping under the trees, running in circles. Though used to moving in various places in ways that deviate from what is the expected norm, there are thresholds for me, always, and the city makes them more apparent. What is appropriate behaviour? What is weird? What is scary? When do people call the police? What do I dare to?

I don't usually practise daring, I depend on a relaxed physicality so that my body can listen, can receive, can react. I don't seek spectacle, I am more interested in integration, in letting site, atmosphere, weather, sink into me, affecting, co-creating my movement.

Soon after installing my magic spell of working from the end, an end point is placed more significantly for my working on site. I am indeed prevented from marking the end of this process with a public performance. Maybe this was to be expected, but I did not expect it. I seem to have misread a friendly thread of emails with the site guardians as an already-yes, which it was not.

The performance found its form anyway, after some wavering and being thrown into this unexpected dilemma. The practice, thankfully, had found its form already then and retained it in its persistent, transparent return.

The world is always present, impacting
upon us. Here, I dance it.
(26.03.2019)

PERFORMANCE

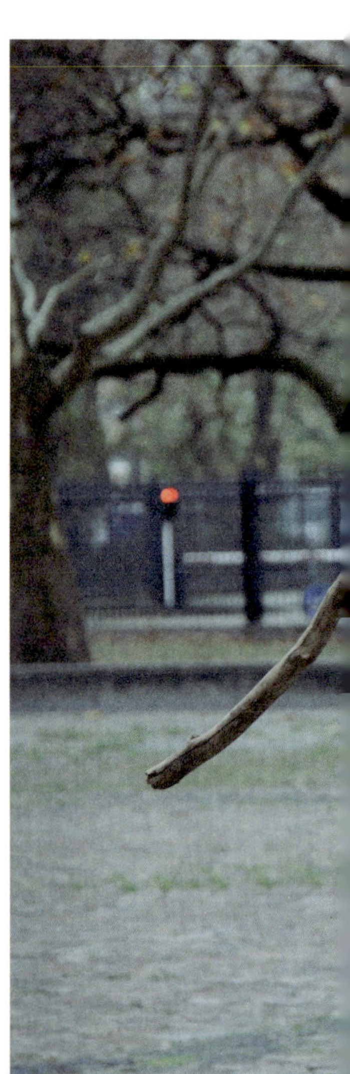

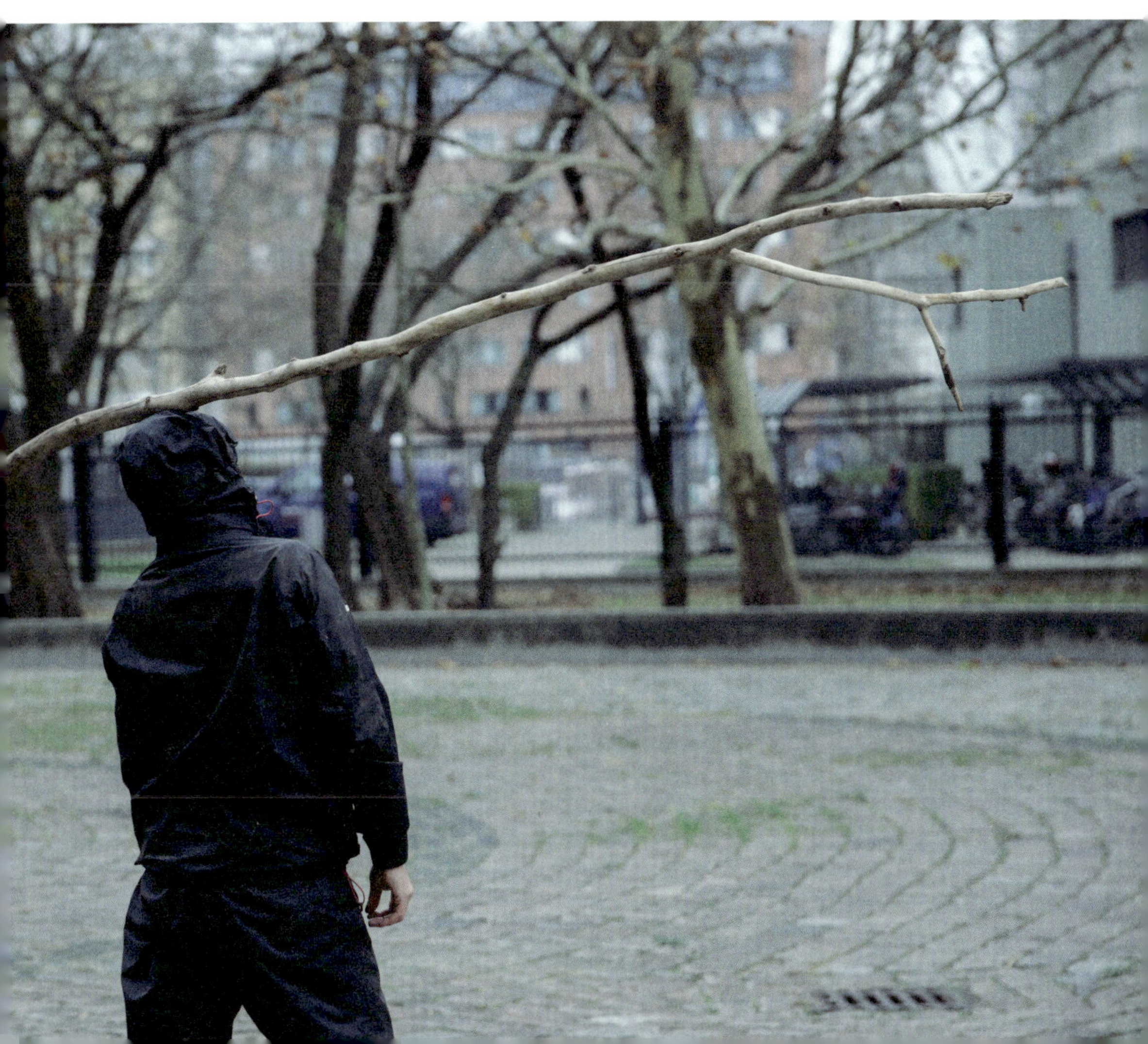

Es kann Ihnen auch auf der Straße keiner
verbieten auf einem Bein zu hüpfen. Out on the
street, no one can stop you hopping on
one leg either.

Ein Vogel fliegt über den Platz und lässt
seinen Schatten da. A bird flies across the
site and leaves his shadow here.
(07.06.2018)

If I attend to texture, can you feel it, also?
(06.04.2019)

This is – Not a Performance

//Paula Kramer

A public performance to close my working process on Südplatz proved impossible for liability reasons. Leading up to the moment when this crucial decision was made, several informal showings had already taken place. And after pondering the situation for a significant amount of time I decided to mark the closure of this work with a performance after all. A performance that wasn't one.

But, first things first.

In May 2017, after the first autumn, winter and spring on site, four 1:1 showings take place, entitled 'Testlauf' ('Trial Run') and organized in collaboration with choreographer Sabine Zahn, who is working-through-roaming in the wider neighbourhood at the time. There are two guests at a time, one walking alongside her, one staying with me and the movements of Südplatz. We exchange visitors, repeat both offerings and meet for a shared chat at the end.

Strawberries and bread, movement and trees, purslane and some rain. There we are, sharing time, space and food, movement and words. One feels the burden of the site in particular, one feels a sense of plasticity in the end. All hear the sounds of the city. "Gentle morphing systems as opposed to violent collisions", writes one.

In a loose succession, peers and colleagues accompany me to this site, as a way of co-experiencing its particular tastes and to support my process of figuring out how to share more widely what this place and my working in it, with it, through it, holds. They are invited to play and stay and witness and bodyguard and document in March and December 2017, and in April and July 2018.

I feel a sense of vulnerability on the site throughout, especially on the open square. But also many moments of strength, playfulness and ease.

> *Es ist doch ganz schön zauberhaft so im kalten, grauen Regen, die Stille hüllt mich ein, ich tauche ein, ganz allein, bin so geschützt in dieser Menschenleere. Tanze irgendwann für die Sehnsucht und nehme den Wind ganz deutlich wahr. It is quite magical in the cold, grey rain, the silence envelops me, and I plunge in, all alone, protected in this empty space. Dancing at some point for a general sense of longing, noticing especially the wind. (30.11.2016)*

> *There is a moment of symphony in which my body can pick up all kinds of qualities [...] the dense strength and curves of the trees nearby, the wind going past, the opening towards Topography. (08.02.2017)*

I begin to wonder if working behind a well-known art institution helps, or if the Pina Bausch exhibition that is showing inside during the first phase of my outdoor meanderings emits good vibes for dancing.

It turns out, however, that working behind a well-known art-institution was what put everything on hold for a while. Working in the shadow of this building also meant working in the shadow of its name. Would I, in a decision-making role, allow uncurated performance activities in 'the back yard'? Maybe. But also, maybe not.

Just as I enter a more intensive, possibly final, rehearsal period, I receive a letter in May 2018, officially prohibiting a public performance here. This happens after a few friendly emails with decision makers, a process of negotiating the possibilities of performing on this particular site. My last call enquiring about the reasons for this letter ends with my being hung up on.

Writing a letter in response re-opens this closed door and a curator from the house agrees to meet with me in June 2018. Whilst I wait downstairs by the porter's office behind the side entrance, I see for the first and only time the many screens with images from the security cameras that I know from outside.

Our meeting comes and goes, uneventful in some ways, yet relevant. The meeting is friendly, there is a sense of sincere interest and concern. The understanding of what bodily practice in conjunction with public space and materials might mean and why this could be relevant is clear. What remains unchanged is that I will not be able to perform on the site. No public announcements, no audience.

From a liability perspective, different institutional bodies (not only Gropius) are responsible for this site; this much I learn. It is problematic to have a group of people on a site that also has lorry traffic unloading exhibition materials – for example. And maybe there were curatorial issues too, maybe not. What to do with this dancer producing art in the back yard? It might have been wiser to ask for permission to work on the site at the very beginning or not at all, but alas – these are thoughts in retrospect.

If I continue to work as I previously have – as a soloist / unannounced / unseen / unscheduled – will this be "a problem", now? The exact margins of what is possible remain blurry. Yet shifting site is not an option (for me). After almost two years, the familiarity and bonds are here. Will what has not bothered anyone in the past, not call for action in the future either? And beyond being able to practise or not: if the work arises differently in the presence of another, but there can be no other, what happens to the work?

Straight after the conversation with the curator I enter the site again.

There is a sense of reconciliation, of belonging to the site again. I count seven trees that protect me, yet my return is tentative at first, just walking. Then also lying, kneeling, moving-dancing. Nothing happens. Just the caretaker of the green spaces who is cutting the roses today and who last time asked if I was OK, says to me as I walk past: "You have been here before, haven't you?" with me answering: "Yes, yes, I am occasionally here, just like you are."

So I return and continue, very slowly, to work on this site. I am easily shaken. I feel vulnerable and surveilled. An added sense of burden and insecurity never fully vanishes again. The conflict leaves traces – it is more difficult now to dance here, disconcerting to become visible – just like before, and more so.

On some level it had always been difficult to work out on the open square. The cameras had always been there. The open arena architecture had always brought a sense of exposure. But a particular sense of belonging, possibility and joy of moving-dancing in and with this public site, forgotten, secluded, protected – had also always been there. Now there is current, specified, concrete friction in the midst of the many layers of challenges, atrocities and changes that are home to this site anyway. I am not only always-already seen, my being here has been challenged.

My throughway is to stay connected to the public aspects of this site. To continue working as I had for two years, visible on all cameras, always; interrupted, never. Conversing with the layers of German history, with politics past and present, with city-trees and daily life, with gardeners and school children, with geocachers and newcomers to this city. With architecture and high skies, animals and plants.

And yet: my flag stays down. I had been on an arc of becoming very visible and I return to camouflage. I stay in conversation, but turn down the volume. I am shaken, this much is clear. But it is possible to return to being a regular item and occurrence on this site and in this way I continue. Never free of doubt, but slowly gaining confidence again.

Almost a year later than originally planned I invite colleagues known and unknown to spend time with me on site, witnessing a ~~performance~~ in the morning hours.

Each invitee receives a letter in preparation, with photos dating from across the three years, some instructions, a bit of scene-setting.

Here, in excerpts:

Berlin, April 2019

Thanks for joining me on Gropius, Südplatz.

I've never before worked in such a complex site, so layered with histories past and occurrences present. Well, I guess all sites are like that, but I've never dealt with it so viscerally (and literally).

Whilst you are on site, I ask you, as much as possible, to not appear as 'audience'. There will only be a few people around and we will only gather as a group at the very end. When you arrive I will already be there, I may have already begun to practise. You begin by arriving and finding a place for yourself (or for you and your 'cohort') - from where you can see, possibly feel, something of what I do. At the same time imagine that you are completely independent of me at this place. (Now this is a difficult combination of tasks and I leave the optimal solution up to you).

On an average day, this site is in moderate use. Some people might sit here, reading a newspaper, having lunch, chatting. People always walk across the square, on their way to work, to 'Topography',

to the wall, to the Federal Ministry of Finance.
Under the trees people with dogs might meander, as
well as geocachers in search of a miniature secret
in one of the trees.

What is important to me is that no obvious 'circle
of viewers' forms. It is equally important that
you can see and feel something, that you can access
the work. Otherwise it all makes no sense.

So far I have never been interrupted, not even
after I have been explicitly asked to not perform.
I respect this agreement, but have been back on
site since, doing things that could be read as a
performance (or not). The practice is reasonably
short (I envision about 30 min.) and despite all
these precursors I invite you to make your viewing
decisions not based on hesitation but on curiosity
and the desire to sense.

A colleague of mine will also be on site and if
questions should come up she will be there to
support me. You could in such a case just witness
what happens and continue with your practice of
not-being-an-audience. Sometimes quite some motion
is happening on the site and sometimes it's so
quiet that a fox crosses it undeterred in the full
diagonal. We will see.

The letter further includes a condensed version of my score (1-3), a verbal map for orientation, as well as questions I sometimes ask myself whilst moving here:

How can I move here, fully aware of the site's historical brutality, its many layers? How can I move here, respecting my own physical condition and the agreements I have made? How can I move here, so that the site's vibrancy and distinctive features can surface and shimmer?

It ends with formalities. Documentation. ~~Performance~~ location. Valediction.

THE SCORE

I've never worked with such an elusive score, catch-me-if-you-can, but this is what it was. Matching the site, the situation, the hovering between appearing-disappearing. I and it – we cannot be held accountable.

PREQUEL

Before anyone is on site with me, I already begin, by the trees, working with a large branch. I kneel, I lean against the bark, I lie down. I am all softness, have to produce nothing. I include in my awareness the presence of the prison and the people who endured exceptional atrocities, behind this fence, right here. I include the weather, the surroundings, the above, the below. I include the bird walking across the site, the grey of the stone, the green of the trees. Very slowly,

I begin.

ONE – under the trees

I lean the large branch against a tree and stand next to another, in a way that allows me to see the thin young tree that is growing up quite straight. I lean and close my eyes.

This has been the place of greatest freedom possible, all along. Here is shelter. The branches have clear shapes and relationships, the trees stand one by one, arranged in their own way. It is easy to be invisible here. Spring is already here, yet the big trees are still winter-bare.

I begin with practising surrender – to this place, to this moment, to the shape of the trees. Their standing, their differences, their arrangement. It tends to be first the bark that guides me, later on my legs might become roots, the branches might form me. My body is shaped by the trees. I enter where I can, I roll and feel and bow, if possible 'in relax', deep relax. I lie with the earth, I follow.

TWO – at the fence

I lean the large branch against the fence, on a diagonal. I stand by the fence. I might walk or turn, touching the fence.

Sometimes the question arises: why can't I turn here? The location of the prison cells is clearly in sight behind / in front of me. Sometimes there is deep grief, even though what happened here happened long ago. Yet in other places people are captured, tortured, abused today – how could this change?

I move mostly in standing, moving slowly towards the open, round plaza. Sometimes there is anger, fear, shame; sometimes there is more sky and wide openness. Softness is almost always there – between the cobblestones are gaps, is earth, is grass; making an inner softness and small collapses possible.

Sometimes the entire surrounding architecture speaks: through clear lines, through might, through reflections, through colours... through bullet holes, through surfaces, through trimmings... through offering context, clarity, form... composition, partnership, resonance. Martin-Gropius-Bau, the grey and stark Ministry of Finance a bit further off, the large world balloon sometimes floating there, the residential buildings behind Topography, the flattened cube of the documentation centre itself, the Europahaus complex... the piece of the Berlin Wall, fences, parking lots... the buildings with many different shapes and the big trees right by Stresemannstrasse, in the distance... sometimes they tell a story, also.

THREE – out on the plaza

I walk away from the fence, crossing the round. Find my place off centre, slightly towards Stresemannstrasse, slightly towards one of the entry ramps going up to what is now the back entrance. I see the long, slightly curved line of the ramp, the cobblestones, the plane trees, the parking lot. I place the big branch on my head and move with it, under it, here. I balance, I turn, I form into forms. I am sheltered under the branch, it is my invisibility cloak. Underneath I can do whatever I want, even out here.

The branch offers weight, offers structure. Sometimes it is more secure on my head, sometimes less. Sometimes it moves, sometimes it falls quickly, sometimes I can turn under it.

I practise becoming structure among structure. Sometimes this allows for a return of freedom. And there is a burden we carry, an obligation we bring to the world, a potential inherent in us. Each person in their own way. As a collective, again in our own way. Something we carry, bring, move. Something that changes.

This is the story I tell with the branch. And further: it is the task of art to keep spaces open. To keep spaces open. Even if everything seems to close, again and again.

Going back through my notes I am especially fascinated by how early on the score already made itself known. A few days into practising it is already clear *that the trees offer protection and a sense of freedom: it doesn't matter so much what I do here. (30.11.2016)* The big branch, the form, the structure, the burden on my back, fell from a tree in May 2017 and I kept it hidden in a corner from then on, digging it out as a movement companion occasionally, not every time. Covered with big leaves, I assume it still to be there. Early on I already carry it on my back as material partner in the face of the open void: *the big open space*

I can only handle (today) with the big branch on my back, reaching far into the back space. (24.11.2017)

The three parts were sometimes five, but already in July 2017 I notate the same three parts and phases of what became 'Not a Performance': under the trees, on the fence, on the square. And *the beginning is under the trees, this much is clear. Der Anfang ist bei den Bäumen, klar. (28.11.2017)*

There were the gaps between cobblestones, offering softness, the bark into which I could enter, the composition of trees to which I could refer, the force of the architecture to which I could respond. What I want to say is: it was all already there. The roots and sources for movement practice, fertile ground for choreography. Waiting to be picked up by my radar, becoming temporarily manifest in my moving, shared and arising anew in the presence of witnesses.

On two days in April 2019 then, I share the work.

The coldness of day one is a pleasure that surprises me. Yet there are fractures, moments of feeling lost. I am momentarily angered by the transient nature of my practice. I stop then, softening inside, inviting site to take over. Some sense of beauty in return, of support, of resonance. Tears by the fence; the grass comes to help me; and under the branch – this moment I really enjoy. To throw myself into becoming structure among structure and through this exploring art-making, dance-making – out here. Speaking to and with and about the burden we all carry, we all bring to life, we all deal with. And the branch slides all by itself from my head onto my shoulder; I note immediately that this will never happen again. And the burden, the task, the gift – is there, just there, all on its own, carried with pride.

On day two a few viewers form a circle after all; a photographer is also with us. The circle is wide and spreads all around the margins of the square. I can see it. Can others? Carefully placed and spaced I see a loose group of some more, some less familiar colleagues. Positioned so particularly, it seems, in the bright spring light – just right. *Frühling – gegen dich bin ich wehrlos. Spring, you make me defenceless,* I note in my diary after the ~~performance~~, *Frühling – gegen dich bin ich wehrlos.* There is a profuse sense of softness within me, a melting inside, during this (thus far) last physical gesture on site. It is incredibly gratifying, partnered with a sense of nothing 'works'. Am I too soft to be precise, too soft to repeat anything planned, too soft for the complex history of this site?

Several of my pathways feel different today. How to speak of the atrocities of Topography in the face of the over-extreme gentleness of spring? I find my way momentarily and there is a strange new movement: standing, my arms and legs crossed, something I have maybe never done before. It feels fitting, between being hung and tied and pulled.

When facing Topography a new feeling arises, a call to approach human atrocities *diagonally* rather than through facing straight on. Something I study, then and there, how to be in the diagonal and therefore maybe more capable of acting or moving, rather than being frozen by a face-to-face confrontation.

The architecture around – not so available; the anger, the sadness – not very present. But I deeply relish lying by the trees at the beginning. And later this being under my branch, as structure, so protected, makes much sense to me. And then I hear the birds above and notice the lines of the branches of the trees. In the end my ability to see is incredibly transformed – I see with heightened precision: the spacing of people, the trees and how everything is placed. We meet under the trees then, in the safe zone, taking a moment to write, each on their own. Then sit in a circle, looking at photographs from across the years, three of which I had included in each letter. Eating some of the landscape. Chatting. It is a gentle conversation that happens in a friendly way. We speak about relevances, but the conversation does not become explanatory. We lightly criss-cross creeks and veins, touching upon: the root of the practice, the why of this place, where/what I might work from, the underlying research, the story of the conflict – and so on.

A place removed from time, an audience member notes. The long shadows of the trees and the wind passing through Südplatz. The traffic noises of the city. The branches of the trees moving with the wind, whilst I balance the branch on my head. A deep, deep sadness of something trapped that wants to escape. And a bee, a very busy bee that flies past, whilst I am still.

"The long gliding descent of a bird into the simulated 'no man's land'. Your movement defied the repetitive gestural mouldings of the Gropius-Bau. Birdsong. The hopeful melancholy of the weak European sunlight. Your expression and carriage were at times determined, like you have a duty or a mission. No foxes." (Joshua Rutter)

Throughout the ~~performance~~ a large shadow triangle crosses the site, like a curtain drawing to a close. The blackthorn is in blossom, once more. I see the wind in the branches and feel a sense of relief that some form of closure was possible, even here.

```
Is it easily identified as "artistic"?
Or do you appear mad?
(audience member, 06.04.2019)


If what you see changes through how I
move, this is it.
(07.06.2018)


What am I doing? I am measuring the
immeasurable. Why? To make visible the
invisible. To maintain and manifest that
every place has more to it than we see.
(08.02.2017)
```

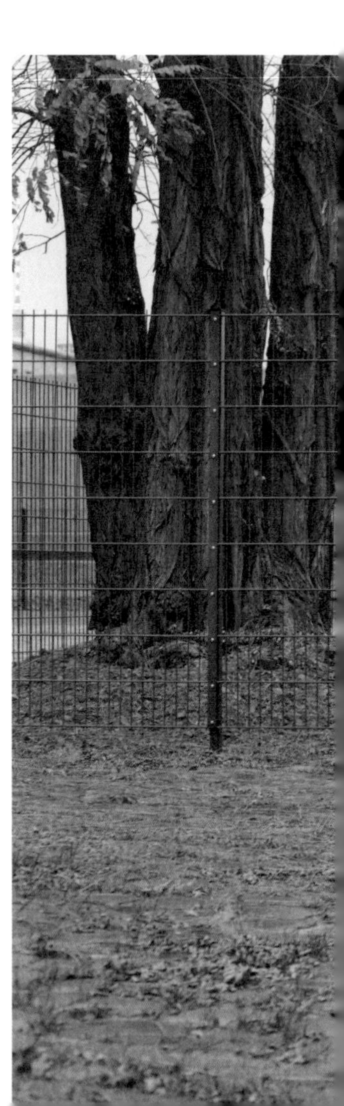

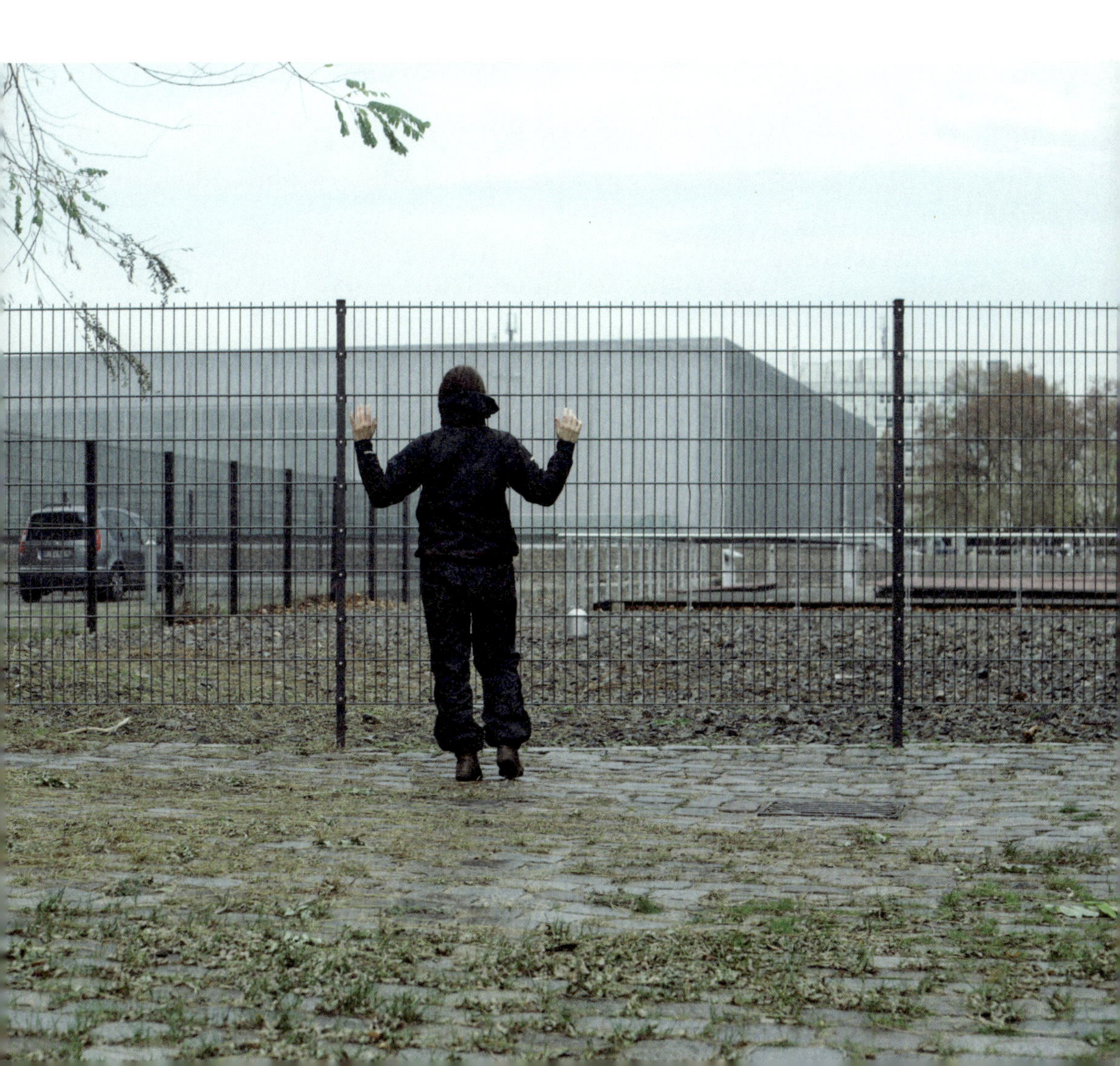

STATE OF MATTER:
Assembled memories of not being an audience

// Jagna Anderson

STILLNESS
AN ANIMAL
PRIMEVAL
    THE BEGINNING.
    GENESIS. AT DAY-BREAK

BIRDS & CARS
NOISE & SILENCE
SILENCE OF THE BODY

It starts with an invitation to a non-performance. The instruction is: not to appear as an audience. As I enter the space behind the Gropius-Bau it is clear, that I don't need to pretend "not being an audience". I am something else. A part of the landscape. A body touching the cold stone, a body immersed in the fresh, crisp air. One of the few human shapes scattered on the margins of the place. The rear of the building seems to be its hidden front. A sense of proud, symmetrical, unneeded frontality with monumental ramp and circular yard is seemingly making passers-by uncomfortable. This is an empty space of exposure and this is not a welcoming stage. There is something very specific about the temperature and the humidity of the air. It glitters in the sunlight, it dips the silhouettes in a soft aura. The space is filled with a vibrating medium of sounds and colours, which seem at the same time very close and very distant.

PERFORMANCE

Bird voices, car engines and tyres, steps. Nothing happens. Everything happens. Something happens. If I say 'something happens' it may suggest that there is a distinct action emerging from the backdrop of stillness. But the contrast between what I perceive at the far south end of the site, in the shade of the trees, and all the other things happening around, is not simply the contrast of movement and stillness, not just a difference of speed, or straightforward-ness or intentionality. I could describe the difference as a difference of density. In the lightness of this morning, in the dispersed vibrations of light, sound and micro-movements, the action of the performer is emerging as something more concentrated, a relative of earth, stone and hard timber. It is denser than the fine grain of birds' voices, the light movement of young tree leaves, the coarse grip of car tyres, as a fish is denser than the water in which it swims. It has a deep temporality of 'ever' and still a freshness of 'beginning'. I feel like I am watching a wild animal, which is at home in its environment. It is just being there and doing things which it has to do. Slow, smooth, heavy, viscous. It invades my evolutionary memory.

REMEMBERED
ENTRAPPED
TORTURED

BURDEN
THE BEASTS OF BURDEN

OUR FRIENDS
WHO ARE GONE AND
THOSE TO COME

There are two: the human and the branch. The performer changed her place, she is in the east now, leaning against a fence and against the sunlight, the long branch shouldered in a way that reminds me of an old milkmaid's yoke, Tragejoch, koromysło. A yoke, an oxbow, a wooden beam. I cannot help it, my fantasy is moving from the primordial forest to the feudal period. At the same time these are just simple materials assembled together: body, timber, metal. Simple architectures of lift, support, balance, suspension. A caryatid. The body of the performer is calm and precise. It contemplates the tiny weight shifts, the contact points between materials. The whole story of being together in the delicate relation of interdependence. Who is a friend and who is a servant? Who is a host and who is a parasite? Who is a tool and who is an agent?

The bare field of the Topography of Terror spreads behind the metal bars of the high fence. Nearby stood the SS prison cells. I cannot see them, but I know, it is not possible not to know. I cannot help but see the figures of the oppressed through the silently moving body of the performer burdened with the dead limb of a tree. My body is scanning its own inherited trauma. I am calling my senses back to the present moment: what I perceive is just an assemblage of body, wood, metal bars. There is the placement in space, the facing, the alignment, the weight, the softness of movement. The body is pregnant. The hair is covered. A pregnant any-body. Gravidity. Gravity. Grave. The caryatid walks towards the middle of the circular space.

LIGHTNESS
    SOFT FOCUS
    DRIFT

          GENIUS LOCI
        WIND NOISE SPIRIT

                THE BRANCH
                  A LIMB
                OF MEMORY

A body can be perceived as a material amongst other materials, a complex biological structure, but still: a matter. Soft, warm, porous, viscous. Or it can be a figure: a tree, an ox, a farmer, a milkmaid, a prisoner. Or it can be somebody: a person, an individual. Or it can be something different, a new entity composed of different materials and shapes. It can branch out a wooden limb: an arboreal human. It can clump and morph with a pavement plate, with the leather of the shoe, the fabric of the pullover. Animal skin and hair meet human skin and hair, plant fibres follow movements of the body, drawing soft, wrinkled lines around it. The body is out of focus: it is almost completely enveloped in those friendly materials. It is a perfect parasite inside its organic cocoon. My eyes follow the gentle line between the beanie and the facial skin. My gaze settles in the plethora of fabric folds. I am amazed by this symbiosis between the moving body and the fabric, between the figure and the costume, between the person and the dress. The body inhabits the textile, the movement inhabits the space. The space inhabits the body. It impregnates it with – pictures from the collective memory: a dancer, a coolie, a runaway, a resistance fighter, a mother.

FABRIC
TEXTILE BODY CASE
    A DISGUISE
        A REMINISCENCE
            IT PASSES BY – IT SLIPS – IT REMAINS
                THE OTHERS
                    I?

I am sharing this experience of non-performance with others, with other members of the small non-audience. Every one of us has a different perspective, every one of us has different memories crossing our minds, every one of us has a different sensation of the crisp air, bright sunlight, cold ground, bird voices, car tyres, pavement slabs. We watch and listen, immersed in our own thoughts and little conversations. We are parts of the same landscape, of the same occurrences. We can see each other. We negotiate subtly the rules of behaving. Sitting or standing, relocating slowly, speaking in soft voices, looking at each other just briefly. After the performance we are a temporary community, sitting together on the ground and sharing food, talking. We put our thoughts on paper. We will go home not knowing what the others have written.

Jagna Anderson // is a Polish-born, Berlin-based performer and artivist. She explores the political agency of matter, body and voice in urban environments. Her work aims at decoding and transforming power relationships in public space by means of participatory research practices, collective interventions, and artist placement. She is a member of several transdisciplinary art collectives and ongoing projects, including p.u.r.e., LAURATIBOR, WAH.

Respect towards the site
Over all sharing the space, being
invited to the site calmed me
down; Last days my body has been
in "alert"-state, being with you and
the site, already the letter ~~to ted~~
a proposed other way of being.
~~the~~ wind and coldness, but at the
same time relaxed, open body
and relation to other beings in
the space.
Pile of sand, traffic light on the
other side, foggy weather, gray
horizon, hazyness in the air (blue),
purple flowers, grass tassels, smells of
~~......~~ soil and "new leafs".
Traffic and workers on the other side
of the gate, security cameras.
Trees, their time.

Text by audience member V.H.

The deadwood resonates *immediately* in
my body, as softness and making/giving space.
(23.07.2018)

On Intermateriality

//Paula Kramer

With the term intermateriality I express my understanding of relationships between, and entwinements of, bodies, sites, senses; objects, materials, histories; atmospheres, weather, feelings – and so on. Intermateriality denotes a confederation or linkage of materials of different orders, a "togethering" (Ingold 2011: 226) that forms part of movement, performance and choreographic practices, as well as daily life. Always already, a kind of baseline happening, but also an event-in-flux that we can notice as well as affect. I suggest that intermateriality is a particularly relevant and fruitful resource for outdoor movement, performance and dance-making, which is why I converse through and with the term in the context of my working practice. Outdoor sites tend to be rich in material diversity and the human body is well equipped to become aware of, and actively involved in, intermaterial happenings. What is otherwise treated as an abstract figure of thought becomes visceral in the context of movement practice.

As a starting point – the very material we are made of is *inter*material. We are, as political theorist Jane Bennett details, always already imbued with tiny living and non-living forms, "[our] flesh is populated and constituted by different swarms of foreigners", not only are we embodied, we are "an array of bodies" (both Bennett 2010: 113, emphasis in the original). Or as feminist philosopher Rosi Braidotti phrases it: our "subjectivity [is] a collective assemblage" (Braidotti 2017: 9).

I previously spoke of intermaterial confederations to articulate "the multi-material and multi-agentic texture of outdoor dancing" (Kramer 2015: 22), drawing primarily on Bennett's work, which invites us to consider seriously the implications of "variously composed materialities that form confederations" (2010: 99). Whilst confederation is a useful term, it is also somewhat alienating in the context of dance and choreography. It speaks first and foremost to and about political entities and their linkages, describing as one example a union formed by states. Whilst I find value in transferring vocabulary in the context of asking how we, as human beings, interlink, interlace, interrelate with the materials, power relations, historical contexts, textures, atmospheres, foods, plants, animals, smells, etc. that share time and space with us, I also search for a vocabulary that resonates best in the context of dance and choreography. Over time I have found that the term intermateriality speaks equally well to what I seek to express, leading more to the core of the matter by becoming subject, rather than being a descriptor, an adjective, an attribute of the noun 'confederation' (or, in variations: relationship, collaboration, linkage and so on).

I position *inter*materiality as *intra*-active in the sense of feminist philosopher and physicist Karen Barad, who suggests that "'environments' and 'bodies' are intra-actively co-constituted" (Barad 2007: 170). However, my work has a different source, emphasis and tuning and I hold on to the prefix *inter-*. Traceable from the Old French 'entre' and the Latin 'inter', *inter-* means "between, among" (COED 2009), making room for separate entities that allow for a between.

It is the common-sensical, the meso-level, the daily life world, that I seek to hold alive and emphasise with this choice of word. This meso-level is particularly relevant in my choreographic practice and the term *inter*materiality is relatively easily understood, also in a non-scholarly context. *Intra*materiality is a viable alternative, however it remains difficult to fathom if one has not already engaged with Barad's work. My position also slightly differs from Barad's argument that "[…] in contrast to the usual 'interaction,' which assumes that there are separate individual agencies that precede their interaction, the notion of intra-action recognizes that distinct agencies do not precede, but rather emerge through, their intra-action" (Barad 2007: 33).

In summary I suggest embarking on a balancing act that acknowledges both deep entanglements and intra-action, as well as valuing separation.

Bodily forms and sensations, choreographic choices and physical movements are co-emergent with site, material, atmosphere – yes. Distinction emerges thought *intra*-action. At the same time, I consider relevant what Barad might call a "preceding" separation, border or differentiation between materials or agencies. It is as basic as considering relevant the approach of a mover towards a site. Whilst always already intra-active, the mover is also coming from elsewhere, from another rhythm and temporality, is made of different stuff than the site, has a different temperature, different intentions. This sense of difference and conscious meeting of differences offers a relevant resource and affects the emergence of movement, score, choreography and/or the character of a performance. To affirm the value of such "preceding" separations and differences, I choose to stay with the prefix *inter-*.

On the whole, however, this choice is a matter of emphasis, brimming with both/and. My concern here is movement practice and choreography, practised and discussed in a way that is grounded in, and fosters, common sense and daily life. Ultimately I suggest that we can emphasize and tune into both the frequency of entanglement as well as the frequency of separation in our living and dancing practices. And at some point we may stop tuning and allow for both (and more) resources to feed our processes of creation, above and below the threshold of what we are consciously able to register.

Intermateriality in Movement Practice

In outdoor movement practice and choreography, intermateriality forms an intricate part of my work. As I physically engage with sites, my moving in time and space emerges through being in relationship with the multi-materiality of the world. I am in constant exchange with the materials, colours, smells, activities, histories of a site. It's a reservoir – always already there, differently available if we choose to attend to it. *[...] the sun made a dramatic difference today, adding shadows, three-dimensionality and texture – I could dance here today, (also) because of the light, because of the space it offered, it created [...]. (26.01.2017)*

At Gropius it was things like the sunlight that touched me on a specific morning, particularly, the availability of the "under earth" or a surprising solidity, tangibility of the space that emerged through snowflakes. One day I suddenly noticed the visible root-system of the trees, "undulating lines" that I returned to many times. As well as the coarse bark that I could slip into and move under, among, with.

On Suomenlinna it was – again, examples – the deep time of rock, the varied colours and textures of the rock surfaces, the co-presence of rock, sea and trees, the wide open sky, ten drops of rain, the presence of animals – that seeped into my body and co-produced my movement.

Your surface meets my surface, your depth meets my depth. Your melted core meets my melting, melted core of trees, I see that too, my perception-timing changes, I move from what I sense, a source becomes clear. Tumbling-melting, being given form, my breathing changes. I breathe out markedly, a little bit like a small machine. Form gives form, I crawl/move at high animal backwards, backwards. (29.05.2018)

All these materials, specific to any site, seep into my body, present themselves through movement, make movement happen. Sometimes the sensation I have is that I enter the material, my feet seem to sink deep into the earth, I slip under the tree's bark and move easily there. At other times, the site-materials enter into my body, the Suomenlinna rock presents itself as a very specific moveable solidity – if I take time for it to permeate my body or if, as above, a melting seeps through me. Layers are relevant here, as is imagination. And sometimes my body makes connections, tells stories from this tree to that one, from that cloud to this rock, from this window sill to that fence – *I weave threads with my hands, draw lines and make connections. (18.05.2017)*

Each particular working time has its particular weather, temperature, atmosphere. The general season and the wider location affects me, as does my constitution, today. The ground I traverse has a specific materiality; densities and structures vary. The sky has particular colours and textures, the soundscape is of a distinct composition, today. I carry with me specific memories and expectations, the places I pass by and where I arrive have specific histories – that I might know of or not – all of which speak. I am, we all are, if we pay attention to this or not, "materially embedded and embodied subjects-in-process [...] [relating] to a multiplicity of forces, entities, and encounters" (Braidotti 2017: 16). It is through practice as well as over time that intermateriality unfolds in a choreographic process – becoming relevant, appearing on its own as well as actively created, noticed and worked with.

What is particularly relevant here, and I draw both on Braidotti and on somatic movement practices, is that we are both "outward bound" (Braidotti 2017: 17) and inwardly attentive. That is, our bodily selves are expanded and relational and part of a "complex field of forces" (ibid.: 16). In addition, as movement practitioners or individuals otherwise interested in attending to bodily states or sensations, we are experienced in tuning into the way we are, feel or are constituted in a particular moment. We are trained to listen to both inside and outside, ideally getting lost in neither realm. These territories are available to, and part of, our awareness, our attending to, our tuning. And if we tune into these resources, if we practise listening to, receiving as well as producing sensorial information on a broad spectrum, intermateriality can become a tangible and supportive resource to work with.

It can begin by noticing something we did not notice before: suddenly another aspect of the site crawls into our consciousness and presents itself as new or relevant. Putting a thread into our hands, which we can choose to follow today. It can begin by touching, body to rock, body to wall, body to tree, body to air and moving from there. It can begin in the past, things we know and don't yet know about the histories and past happenings on a site seep into our bodies, influencing our imagination, movements, associations.

These processes take place anyway and at the same time we can augment them. We can prepare our bodily material and work in regular exposure to sites. We can tune all sensorial faculties available to us and make space in our bodyminds for materials to speak to us. We can make bodily contact, receive the site and follow.

The works on both Suomenlinna and Gropius's Südplatz were composed like that. In multiple, intimate, recurrent conversations between bodies and materials of different orders. In *intermateriality*. The excerpts from my movement diaries above, as well as the many different episodes mentioned elsewhere in this book, speak to and about such experiences and practices of existing-in-intermateriality.

May these, as well as your own, inspire future choreographic processes as well as invite practising a "new, subtler, and more complex relationship to our planetary dimension" (Braidotti 2017: 10) more generally. Living and dancing not only in and with an ethics of care for self and other, but actively-receptively positioned in a living field of many; co-composed by and co-composing with all that shares time and space with us.

References:

Barad, Karen (2007): *Meeting the Universe Halfway: Quantum Physics and the Entanglement of Matter and Meaning.* Durham, NC: Duke University Press.

Barad, Karen (2012): 'On Touching – The Inhuman That Therefore I Am (v 1.1)'. [online] https://www.are.na/block/1799783

Bennett, Jane (2010): *Vibrant Matter: A Political Ecology of Things.* Durham and London: Duke University Press.

Braidotti, Rosi (2017): 'Posthuman Critical Theory' in *Journal of Posthuman Studies*, Vol. 1, No. 1, pp. 9-25.

Concise Oxford English Dictionary COED (2009), edited by Catherine Soanes and Angus Stevenson.

Ingold, Tim (2011): *Being Alive: Essays on Movement, Knowledge and Description.* London: Routledge.

Kramer, Paula (2015): *Dancing Materiality. A Study of Agency and Confederations in Contemporary Outdoor Dance Practice*s. PhD Thesis. Coventry University, Centre for Dance Research.

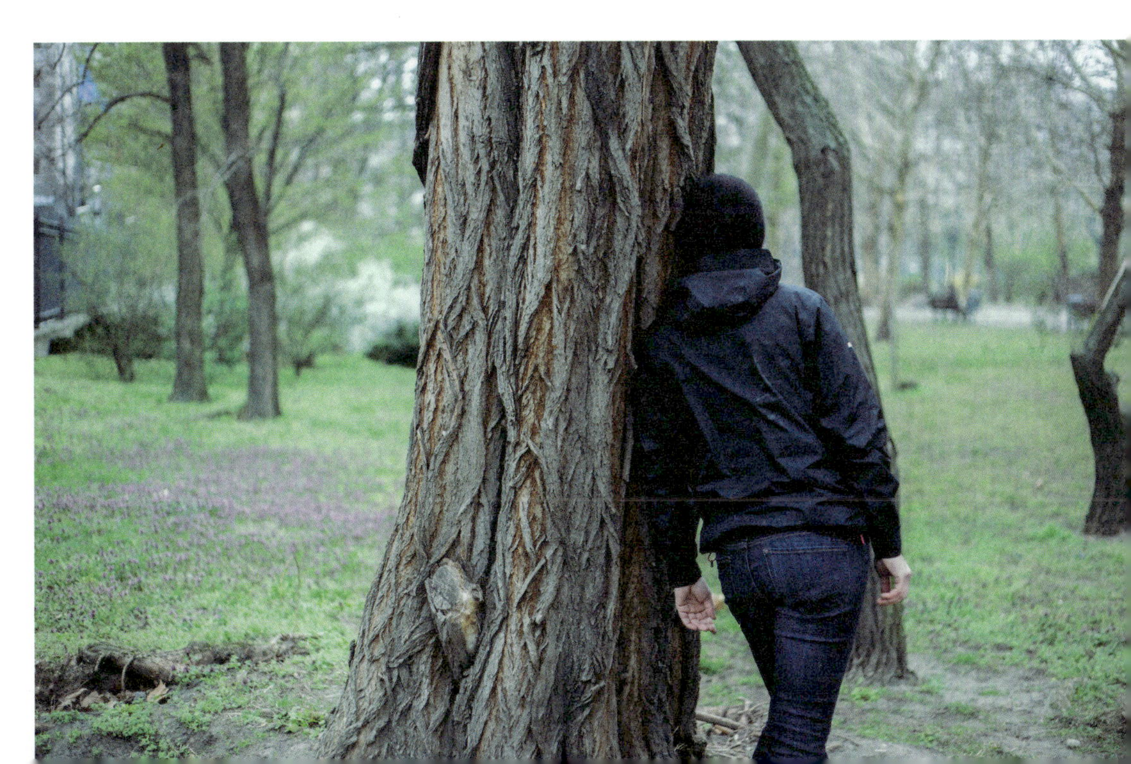

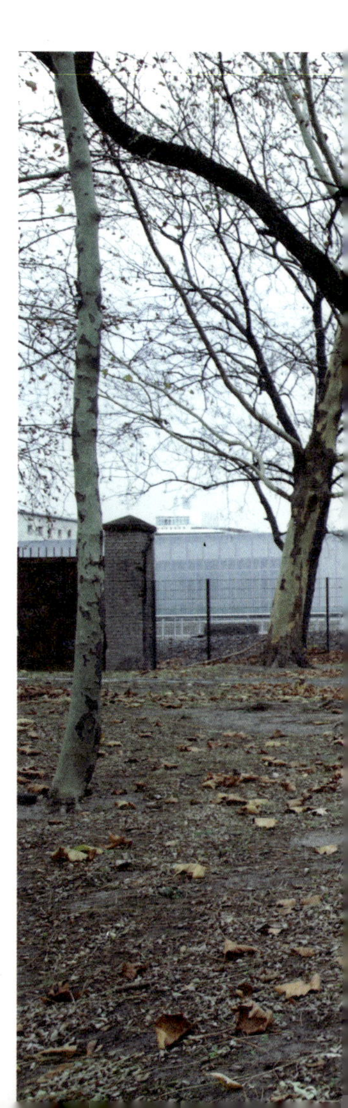